M000290294

"Adam Contos is a strong and confident communicator whose determination, boldness, and successes have helped him truly understand what it means to be a leader today. The same leadership capabilities enabled his successes across diverse and distinctly different career paths—street cop, SWAT team leader, and now RE/MAX. Listen to what he has to say."

**—Barbara Kreisman, PhD, Professor Emerita and Associate Dean of Daniels College of Business, University of Denver, and partner, Intergistic Solutions Management Consulting**

"In the remarkably actionable and relatable *Start With a Win,* Adam Contos reframes the outdated view of success as an often daunting 'destination,' to a series of achievable 'wins' that propel you toward your self-determined goals. Contos offers a real-world roadmap to move past the inevitable challenges we all face, while providing frequent dopamine hits to fuel your journey. It's a fresh take on leadership that deserves attention. Highly recommended."

**—David Avrin, president, The Customer Experience Advantage, and author of *The Morning Huddle* and *Why Customers Leave (and How to Win Them Back)***

# START WITH A WIN

# START WITH A WIN

## TOOLS AND LESSONS TO CREATE PERSONAL AND BUSINESS SUCCESS

### ADAM CONTOS

WILEY

For general information on our other products and services or for technical support, please contact our Customer Care Department within the United States at (800) 762-2974, outside the United States at (317) 572-3993 or fax (317) 572-4002.

Wiley publishes in a variety of print and electronic formats and by print-on-demand. Some material included with standard print versions of this book may not be included in e-books or in print-on-demand. If this book refers to media such as a CD or DVD that is not included in the version you purchased, you may download this material at http://booksupport.wiley.com. For more information about Wiley products, visit www.wiley.com.

*Library of Congress Cataloging-in-Publication Data is Available:*

ISBN 9781119807070 (Hardback)
ISBN 9781119807094 (ePDF)
ISBN 9781119807087 (ePub)

Cover Design: Wiley
Cover Image: © Magic marker; © Ron Dale/Shutterstock, arrows/circles;
©TWINS DESIGN STUDIO/Shutterstock

SKY10029078_083121

*To my wife and best friend, Kelly. I love you forever.*

# Contents

# CONTENTS

# Introduction

**L**ook in the mirror and make the conscious choice to say, "I can." Congratulations. You're on the way to your first win.

Whatever you want to achieve in business and in life, the first step is believing in yourself. You choose to take control of your life—to succeed. That's not motivational-speak; that's *real* life. Wins begin with believing "I can" instead of embracing the excuses why you cannot.

I changed my own attitude and approach, and went from being a two-time college dropout to a street cop, deputy sheriff, SWAT team leader, and now CEO of a large multinational public holding company, the real estate industry giant RE/MAX.

A win isn't defined by dollars and cents or a destination; it's a journey—a series of experiences—that, done right, brings happiness along the way. No matter the business or the situation, a win simplified is a group of answers to these questions:

- What is the challenge?
- What is the necessary attitude to get started?
- What action or actions are necessary to overcome the challenge?

Whoever you are, whatever your circumstances, whatever your business, each of us has the power to transform our lives and the lives of those around us. We can learn to lead and strive to win in all we do; or we can take the easy way—follow the herd, accept our circumstances, and never achieve our potential. Whether the goal is to improve relationships in business or in our personal lives, the choice is ours to make every day.

This isn't a book about the mechanics of buying and selling real estate. This is a playbook to help you learn how to lead—to lead yourself and lead others. In turn, that leadership creates business and opportunities to do business because people understand that leaders are problem-solvers who get things done and done right.

Each day is a new opportunity to either choose to win or opt to embrace fear and approach the day with "I can't." Which viewpoint will you take?

Business is no different. With the onset of the pandemic and quarantine in early 2020, the real estate industry, like so many others, all but shut down. Transactions screeched to a halt. RE/MAX had two choices: do nothing and ride it out, or address the challenges and look for opportunities. We chose the latter. Many franchises and agents relied on artificial intelligence data to assess the marketplace and on virtual tours and video links to connect with clients. These leaders found a way to make it happen instead of sitting on the sidelines and watching their businesses fall apart.

In these pages, I'll share with you the playbook to create your own wins. You'll learn the fundamentals and actions required to gain the necessary skills and confidence to transform your life. I'll share stories with practical applications and suggestions on how you, too, can start with a win.

Life is a series of missions—experiences and interactions—that shape who we are and how we respond to situations and people. Whether positive experiences or learnings (the not so positive experiences), missions lay the framework for the playbook of life. Every mission matters; it's an opportunity to learn and grow. When we think about a mission's specifics, we are psychologically training ourselves in how to respond to a similar situation in the future.

Within each mission we take actions, which are the solutions to the challenges. Those solutions become part of our playbook of life.

This book will help you learn why dealing with your emotions—especially fear—often sets the playing field for a mission win or not. I'll share how every interaction and every mission is a learning experience. I spent two years on the streets of metropolitan Denver, Colorado, as an undercover narcotics cop buying drugs *and* perfecting my marketing skills. Those missions amounted to my own sales and marketing class, which I refer to as Narc Marketing 101—some of the best sales training possible.

*Start With a Win* will also help you better understand the importance of sharing your knowledge and allowing others to share their wisdom with you. As an off-duty deputy sheriff working a side job, I met my business mentor in the middle of the night on a golf course under construction at the base of the Colorado mountains. He helped me understand step by step how to be a great business leader. I'll share that same knowledge with you. Each chapter will include insights as well as personal stories and takeaways you can use in the quest for your own wins.

Don't let anyone tell you, "You can't." You can! Now let's head out on your journey.

# PART I

# IT'S YOUR CHOICE

## CHAPTER 1

## Attitude: You Can!

*"A rut is nothing more than a shallow grave."*[1]

**L**ook in the mirror and make the decision to say, "I can." Congratulations, you're on your way to win No. 1.

Whatever you want to accomplish in life, no matter the naysayers or the doubters, the roadblocks or the fears, the uncertainties or the challenges, the first step to achievement is believing in yourself. In business and your personal life, you make the conscious choice to win—to succeed—every day. It's the decision to commit to taking control of your life and your happiness.

That's not motivational-speak; it's the truth from a real-ologist. Your success depends on believing the "I can" instead of coming up with excuses to justify the "I don't have to."

I know; I changed my own attitude and approach and went from being a street cop in a sleepy suburb of Denver, Colorado, to being a deputy sheriff, SWAT tactical commander, and now CEO of a

---

[1] *Asbury Park Press* (Asbury Park, NJ, 1973), p. 48.

large multinational public holding company, the real estate industry giant RE/MAX.

*The first step to a win is to make your latest excuse your last one.*

## UNDERSTANDING A WIN

A win isn't defined by dollars and cents or a destination; it's a journey—a series of missions or experiences—that, done right, bring happiness along the way. No matter the business or the situation, a win is simply a set of answers to these questions:

- What is the challenge?
- What is the necessary attitude to get started?
- What action or actions are necessary to overcome the challenge?

Whoever you are and whatever your business or circumstances, you have the power to transform your life and the lives of those around you. Each of us can choose to lead by overcoming challenges, creating solutions that help others, and then turning those solutions into consistent actions. The framework is the same whether the challenge is to win a football game, close a sale, or build a business. Leaders create a plan, include great people, turn the plan into actionable steps, and influence the execution of the plan. Leaders create opportunities and grow businesses, too, because other people recognize leaders who solve problems and get things done.

A win really is that simple—challenge, attitude, actions. So often we complicate winning and make it overwhelming. Instead, step back and understand the simplicity. We can win, and you can, too.

*Lack of action = lack of results (always)*

We can learn to lead and strive to win in all we do, or we can take the easy way—follow the herd, accept our circumstances, and never achieve our potential. The choice is ours.

> *"There are two types of people who will tell you that you cannot make a difference in this world: those who are afraid to try and those who are afraid you will succeed."*
>
> —Ray Goforth, executive director of the Society of Professional Engineering Employees in Aerospace

## Your Opportunities

Every day is a new opportunity, a new choice to start again. Faced with challenges, you can choose to turn that day into a win. Or you can opt to excuse yourself, embrace fear, and think instead, "I can't," "no way," "but," "impossible." Of note: The word "but" is the beginning of a rationalized excuse. Don't use it.

## Go for the Win

It's like the bison and the cow. Bison instinctively know that charging into a storm gets them through and out of the weather more quickly, while cows turn away and drift with the wind, sometimes dying in the process.[2]

In business it's no different. Think positively, embrace your inner bison, and head into the storm—face the problem head on and go for the win. The true test of leadership—your own and others'—is how you respond when you get punched in the face. Do you step up, stay present, deploy kindness and gratitude, and face the challenges with confidence and transparency? Or do you hide?

### THE WINNING APPROACH
*In the face of a challenge, winners:*

- *Step up.*
- *Stay present.*
- *Deploy kindness and gratitude.*
- *Face the challenges with confidence and transparency.*

---

[2]National Bison Association. "The Bison Advantage."https://bisoncentral.com/the-bison-advantage/

# MAKING THE RIGHT CHOICE

With the onset of the COVID-19 pandemic in early 2020, many companies questioned their survivability. The real estate industry came to a grinding halt. We couldn't physically go into other people's homes; transactions stopped abruptly. Some homebuyers in the middle of the purchase process even found themselves homeless.

But the lockdown presented new opportunity for those people, companies, and leaders willing to dig deeply into the challenges and find ways to progress, accelerate, and adapt. RE/MAX recognized that our business had taken on a life-essential urgency for some people. We had two choices: do nothing or devise new ways to address the roadblocks, take action, and overcome the problems.

We locked our physical doors and went virtual March 13, 2020. Our executive team's first virtual meetings were scary—all gloom and doom because we knew our cash would last less than a year. We also recognized that, as a public company, we had to maintain value for our shareholders and keep our franchisees' companies solvent.

We resolved to refocus our leadership and solve the problems because hundreds of thousands of people were looking to us for solutions. Among the questions we faced:

- How do we reopen for business when we can no longer follow our usual procedures?

- How do we reconnect with our customers when their new mindset is "closed for business"?

- How do we manage a public company's budget when cash flow stops?

The fear and stress facing our leadership team—and so many tens of thousands of other companies—turned into action as we explored our opportunities. After all, when faced with challenges, leaders create opportunities. We stepped up and provided answers for our company, our franchisees, our shareholders, and ourselves.

## LEADERS LEAD

Leading is not only about making decisions and taking actions; it's also about creating positive motion—physical, emotional, and professional—in the lives of others.

## E-CONNECTIONS

As the franchisor and holding company, we turned to virtual connections. We offered guidance and technical assistance, video tutorials and training, and step-by-step suggestions for how to address remote sales and marketing. Most importantly, though, we were present and ready to help.

Our franchisees quickly adapted with us because we were all aligned through our culture of a business that builds businesses—even in challenging times. Leveraging our great relationships, we headed into the storm together and pursued opportunities. We all moved quickly. Many of our franchisees and agents turned to the artificial intelligence (AI) data we provided to assess the marketplace. They then used virtual tours and video connections to work with clients, and all with COVID-safe protocols in mind.

Despite the complexities in what at the time was uncharted territory, we sought and embraced the opportunities and came away with a big win, helping plenty of people in the process. Despite advice from many to do so, RE/MAX didn't lay off anyone in 2020. In fact, we saw opportunities and acquired two new companies: Gadbery Group, a geospatial data provider, and Wemlo, a loan processor. The year 2020 was one of our company's best because we consciously chose to assess the situation, face the challenges, and take the necessary actions to solve the problems.

## SPA FOR THE WIN

The formula for the win is simple. Whether a business involves real estate, sales, marketing, banking, negotiating, creating, or almost anything else, problems can be solved with SPA. That's an acronym for Stress, Planning, Action—the three steps to results. It works in your personal life, too.

Stress is created when a problem surfaces. It's an energy that, if harnessed, can be used for benefit or, if left to stew uncontrolled, ends up a detriment. It's a tension each of us creates within ourselves. To use the stress wisely takes planning to assess the problem and create solutions. And it takes action to carry out the plan to solve the problem.

Try approaching a problem with SPA. Follow through on *every* step, and you'll be closer to starting with a win every time. Fail to act, and your problems could consume your life.

## TAMING THE BEAST—YOUR EMOTIONS

Long before I took the helm of RE/MAX, I was crippled by fear, unsure of what I wanted and willing to let opportunities sail past. Does this sound familiar? I allowed the excuses and the "I can't" to control my life. I graduated high school and the next day joined the Marines. I'm a college dropout—twice—with poor grades, too.

## EXPERIENCE THE WINS

One day I realized that wins, or lack thereof, were up to me. I could stay lost in the herd, on life's treadmill, controlled by my fear and emotions—the Beast within (more on that later). Or I could make my own difference, learn to tame the Beast, and turn my experiences into wins.

That wake-up call happened when I was a deputy sheriff working primarily domestic violence cases. Even though I wasn't willing to admit it at the time, the negative energy swirling around me every day had started to take a toll. I was burning out on my job. One day a colleague asked if I was OK. That was my aha moment; I realized that I wasn't OK and that I needed to do something about my situation—take action (think SPA)—before the negativity consumed me.

When stress and negativity surround us, we start to believe it. The negativity can come from a job, relationships, or even the daily news. Too often people realize they're trapped in negativity and fail to take action; the negativity proves overwhelming and takes control of their lives. Often, it feels like it's easier to ignore what's happening and allow a situation to smolder rather than do something about it. Wrong! It's just as easy to take action to improve your life as it is to allow your life to decline. The hardest part, though, is deciding that you have had enough and want to switch to the course of positivity—to the mindset of "I can."

## LOOK UP, NOT DOWN

Relationships—business or personal—with yourself or others all matter. We need to deal with them, not ignore them, to find success in all aspects of our lives. Think of a relationship that's not working as a crack in a wall. With added pressure, that wall will eventually collapse.

The negativity and stress associated with the domestic violence cases I worked day in and day out had cracked my wall and threatened to collapse it. The problem wasn't the work. It was the attitude that I had allowed myself to develop. I had decided that because I was dealing with misery, I should be miserable, too. I was there to help others, not hurt myself. Fortunately my colleague noticed and said something. I just needed someone—my colleague—to wake me up to the reality. I needed to take action to make a change, and I did.

Soon after that realization, RE/MAX founder and friend Dave Liniger provided the wisdom I needed to move on: *People need to be in an environment where they can be as successful as they want—where they look up instead of down.*

I learned to redirect my fears, embrace "I can," accept the challenges, be a leader of myself and others, and take action. I also learned that each of us has to take care of ourselves. Why? Because if you're stuck, you can't possibly help others get unstuck. Think about the safety briefing on an airplane, which reminds passengers before takeoff: "In the event of cabin depressurization, the oxygen masks will fall . . . place it over your nose and mouth and breathe normally . . . once you have secured your mask, you may help others around you."

The deeper meaning is that in order to help others, each of us must help ourselves first. Too often people try to help others when, in reality, they need help themselves.

## THE SKY IS YOUR LIMIT

Since I rebounded from burnout, I've been a SWAT team leader and entrepreneur. I started an online police supply company in the 1990s and then formed a security consulting firm not long after that. I earned an MBA, and today I helm RE/MAX, one of the world's largest companies. You may recognize us from our red, white, and blue hot-air balloons that dot the skies across the country and around the world. We have more than 140,000 agents in more than 8,700 offices across 110 countries and territories. RE/MAX is in the business of selling real estate and mortgage franchises, sharing information, offering mortgages, providing guidance, and, above all, helping people believe in themselves and become better at what they do.

I didn't initially build the company—Dave Liniger and his RE/MAX team did that. But I've worked with the company since 2004, helmed it since 2018, and in the process helped many others find their own wins along the way. I say that with great humility because sometimes all it takes is a small tailwind, a slight change in attitude and approach, and you, too, can score a win.

## LOCUS OF CONTROL

During tough times, we make the conscious effort not to level blame but rather to head into the storm, face the problems, come up with the solutions, and take action. Any leader who blames someone else for anything is not leading; they are blaming. It's back to the "I can" versus the excuses why not.

Human nature dictates that we level blame against a person as opposed to a process. However, blaming a person is an attack that diverges from solving the problem. Before laying blame, think about what your internal problems are. Anyone can lay blame, but not everyone has the fortitude and balance to lead across all aspects of their lives. Great leaders fix problems instead of placing blame.

## OWNING THE OUTCOMES

Any of us can achieve that balance if we take ownership of outcomes. The psychology behind the concept is a version of *locus of control*. Developed in 1954 by Julian B. Rotter, PhD, locus of control refers to whether we take ownership of outcomes or make excuses and blame others.[3]

Someone who praises or blames external factors for outcomes exhibits external locus of control. You lost the game because it rained. Not your fault, right? Wrong! You lost the game because your opponent outplayed you that particular day regardless of the weather. Conversely, people with an internal locus of control take ownership of outcomes. You did poorly on an exam or didn't achieve your sales goals, for example, so you recognize that you didn't prepare enough or that you didn't lay the right groundwork. You own the fact that the results are up to you.

In other words, your locus of control determines the degree to which you feel you have control over your results and ultimately your life. You can either own the results regardless of outside forces, or you can blame them on outside forces and be the perennial victim.

---

[3]Bonnie R. Strickland, "Julian B. Rotter, 1916–2014," *American Psychology* 69 (Jul–Aug 2014): 545-6. DOI 10.1037/a0036918. PMID: 25046717; National Center for Biotechnology Information, National Library of Medicine, National Institutes of Health, https://pubmed.ncbi.nlm.nih.gov/25046717/.

# FOUNDATION FOR LEADERSHIP, BALANCE

Locus of control is holistic across all parts of life. It's a foundational aspect of leadership, too. We can achieve a holistic and healthy approach to life with ownership of outcomes. Locus of control is the beginning of balance because each of us must be in charge of how we choose to operate and what outcomes we create.

Ultimately, we can't pick and choose when to be a leader and when not to be. Leaders lead across all aspects of their lives. Constantly and consistently, they create wins and learn from losses in everything they do.

# YOUR TURN

Which locus of control do you have? Think about this for a moment. What do you believe when it comes to your outcomes?

Do you blame someone or something else for negative results? Are your financial issues the fault of society or someone else? Is the amount of money you make your doing or someone else's? Is your poor health the fault of the food engineer at the potato chip factory or the ice cream shop down the street? Are your weight issues and back pain the fault of the couch manufacturer?

If you answered "yes" to any of the above questions, you should thank your boss for doing your job for you so you can collect a paycheck. So many people blame others when the fault is their own. If you feel like a victim of society and you can't do anything about it, again, that's external locus of control. Conversely, if you understand that you get what you get but you will do everything you can through your own actions to make that outcome the best one possible—with comfort in the risk even if it doesn't come out in your favor—that's internal locus of control. I view internal locus of control as expending energy, effort, and focus on the project, and not on excuses or criticisms.

## LEADERSHIP QUALITY

Leaders generally have a strong internal locus of control; they use any situation to learn and adapt rather than lay blame. It's OK not to succeed at something; it's not OK as a leader to blame something or someone else. When you believe you can always impact the outcome—internal locus of control—you will learn as much from negative outcomes as positive ones and be more likely to overcome failures. There will be problems and fails; that's OK as long as you understand it's all part of the process of getting better.

So many people in life try to blame shortcomings, missed opportunities, or failures on something other than their own actions, or lack thereof. Those same people try to take credit for their successes. You can't have it both ways!

## TAKE ACTION

We've all at some point hesitated to take action out of fear—the Beast within each of us. Maybe you identified an ideal sales prospect but hesitated to make the cold call, or you were invited to address an audience and backed out.

Rather than freeze with inaction, a leader uses that fear as a reason to act, to do something about the situation. A leader fires off that email, picks up the phone, knocks on the door, walks to the podium, and embraces the crowd without a second thought. Successful people take action when others don't.

## A ROOKIE COP

In the early 1990s, I was a rookie reserve police officer in Cherry Hills Village, an upscale community in south Denver. I was in training working the night shift when we received an alarm from a local megachurch—one of those with a huge sanctuary that holds hundreds of people. My training sergeant, Pat, and I immediately responded, along with two other squad cars.

The building's caretaker met us on-site and unlocked the church door. By now, we figured this was probably a false alarm—perhaps a bird inside the sanctuary had set off an alarm sensor. We walked around inside briefly without seeing anything unusual.

I decided to take one more lap around the sanctuary and told the other officers I would meet them at the front entrance. I began to walk from the back down one of the long aisles that converges at the pulpit. Suddenly the hair on the back of my neck bristled; my stomach knotted. I could hear the silent voice in my head yelling, "Something is wrong, take action!" As a rookie, I had never been in an armed confrontation, but my subconscious survival instinct must have kicked in. (Pay attention to those instincts, or an opportunity to take action can pass by.)

Over my right shoulder I saw what I thought was a leather purse on a seat. Then that silent voice yelled, "Put a gun in your hand, now!" I drew my weapon, spun around, and pointed it at the face of a man emerging from where I thought the purse had been. He was climbing to his feet and had a silver object that in the dim light looked like a knife. He was so close that I almost shot him right there. (Law enforcement are taught that a knife-wielding assailant can close a 21-foot gap and stab you before you can even react.)

I was scared even though the weapon he was holding turned out to be a silver nail file. He had used it to try to break into the church's cash box; that's what had set off the alarm. I tried to radio for help, but the signal couldn't penetrate the sanctuary walls. We both stood there; he looked at me with that "Now what?" stare.

I knew I had to act, so nervously I ordered him to drop the knife or I would shoot. Thankfully, he complied. He was probably as startled and afraid as I was. What seemed like an eternity passed as I held him there at gunpoint. I think it was actually only a few seconds before my partners showed up. Veteran cops, they handcuffed the man, then gave me a high-five and hugs for catching my first felony in progress.

# WINS FOLLOW A PROCESS

That night's mission was a win. I faced the challenge, examined the options, and fortunately, without hesitation, took the actions necessary to safely solve the problem. That night also illustrates how a street cop can end up as CEO of a megacorporation.

Whatever the challenge, to solve the problem takes the right attitude and approach to *every* mission. That includes:

- Recognize the challenge or challenges.
- Meet the people involved who don't know or trust you.
- Gain their trust and confidence through your attitude and actions.
- Solve the problems.

# THE POWER OF LEADING, NOT FOLLOWING

Actions got me to where I am today, but I promise you, those missions and those actions came with plenty of fear. That's a cost of moving forward in pursuit of wins.

*"We generate fears while we sit. We overcome them by action."*[4]

—Henry Link, PhD (1889–1952), psychologist

That night in the church I was scared, but I wasn't petrified. I took action because I knew I had to. I had prepared well for this, having spent long hours practicing building searches and tactical techniques, understanding potential threats on the job, and talking through all of this with my trainers.

There is a first time for everything in life; don't let that scare you away. Whether a challenge is business-related or personal, we all can

---

[4]Henry C. Link, *My Return to Religion* (Morrisville, NC: Lulu.com, 2011).

learn to conquer the fear (the Beast) and earn the win by approaching problems holistically, one step at a time. That's part of being a leader.

In any situation, leaders:

- Assess the situation or the problem and ask themselves, "What is the question that needs to be answered?"
- Answer the question and fix the collapsed points, including weaknesses in the framework.
- Understand the options available and prepare for action.
- Move forward for the win.

## IDENTIFY PROBLEMS FIRST

While a deputy sheriff, I also was a part-time entrepreneur. One of the businesses I started was a security consulting firm. At the time, the early 2000s, real estate agents were being increasingly victimized—robbed, assaulted, sexually assaulted, and even murdered while doing their jobs—which was the problem I was addressing. I examined the situation and identified the security vulnerabilities they faced (assessed the problem), looked more closely at the situation, and theorized that the reasons agents were targeted—the collapsed points—included their lack of training or focus on safety. Primarily, many were unaware of their available options if they encountered bad situations, or they didn't know how to avoid them altogether and still do their jobs. They were meeting unknown people in unfamiliar places and not building any avoidance or response options into the process. Agents essentially were going where the police wouldn't go without protection, training, or a partner.

So my company came up with the answer—S.A.F.E.R. (Safety Awareness for Every REALTOR©)—a program that taught individuals the four fundamental concepts of personal safety: awareness, avoidance, de-escalation, and response if action is required.

Eventually I pitched S.A.F.E.R. to RE/MAX, and it was a big hit. More importantly, the solution helped others. S.A.F.E.R. was also my introduction to the real estate and franchising industry. I traveled around North America, speaking to agents and brokers and learning about their industry and challenges. It turned out that many of their challenges weren't safety issues; rather, they were business issues that put them in poor safety situations. Remember, success lies in deconstructing the challenges into smaller, more manageable pieces, and then fixing the problems one at a time.

About a year after instituting the S.A.F.E.R. program, RE/MAX asked me to join the company as a franchise consultant. It meant a pay cut and leaving law enforcement—at the time I was a SWAT leader—as well as trying something new and different. Momentarily my Beast—fear of the unknown—reared its head. Others told me I was making a big mistake by leaving law enforcement. But I believed in my abilities, as did my friend and mentor Dave Liniger. I also recognized that, at best, this move could be a new career and, at second best, an incredible learning experience. Beast be damned.

## EXPECT THE FEAR

The first time I addressed a large crowd—1,500 people—I was nervous and a little afraid. I understood suddenly why so many people are afraid of public speaking. Like many public speakers before they go on stage, I worried about a number of issues: whether people would listen to me, whether they would care about what I had to say, whether my message would be clear, whether I would embarrass myself, and all those other little and not-quite-so-little fears that can nag at each of us.

**A mission.** But I approached my speech as another mission, and that enabled me to separate it from my fear—the Beast. It's the same approach I used as a SWAT officer or on a sheriff's call. I had a script and I knew the mission; I had practiced the speech many times, and so I walked on stage confident that I could do the job right, and I did.

Nearly two decades and literally thousands of presentations later, I still get a little nervous. I consider it my quality-control awareness. But today, just as then, I know my material, practice my presentation over and over and over again, and address people I care about, so my words come across as genuine and caring. Admittedly though, my speeches are a little more comfortable and conversational now as opposed to those early speeches.

Everyone thinks there's a secret to public speaking, but there's not. Faced with presenting, follow the principles above for a win. Repeated practice is essential to familiarize yourself with the content. Too many people try to script too many things. But audiences don't want a scripted talk. They don't want you to read; they prefer a free-flowing conversation, which requires knowledge of the ideas so they can be shared easily, freely, and comfortably.

It's the same procedure for video presentations. Audiences want to hear and see confidence, a positive attitude, and kindness or caring.

**Study and practice.** I learned to improve my speech delivery by reading how great public speakers do it. I also watched videos of other amazing public speakers—not for the content or the delivery methodology, but for the tone, tempo, delivery, and how the speaker reads their audience. It's called public speaking and not public talking for a reason. You're communicating as if you're having a two-way conversation, only the feedback from the crowd is in their response, not their words.

**Seek comment.** Feedback from a presentation also allows us to continually learn and improve. Despite all the speeches I've made over the years, I still seek out and appreciate feedback after every speech or presentation. I have had speaking consultants critique my work and rip it apart. It hurts to hear your mistakes, but you listen, learn, and improve. I also review video or audio of my presentations. I don't like to watch myself present—I don't think anyone does—but I do it to see if there are ways I can improve for next time.

Reviewing the product of your work is important in whatever we do, whether it's a speech, a sale, a document, or a mission in your life. When my wife and I leave the gym in the morning, we even discuss our workouts and how to make them better—or we celebrate our victories.

If we ignore pursuing excellence in one thing, we ignore it in everything. That goes for shooting a two-minute video on social media all the way to standing in front of 10,000 people to deliver a speech.

## WINNING IN UNCERTAIN TIMES

Uncertainty is *the* certainty in business and in life. We grow the fastest when we win in uncertain times. Our ability to recover from failure and our ability to lead grows too. I've learned firsthand.

Several years after joining RE/MAX full time, we faced an economic crisis. Dave pulled me aside and told me this would be the hardest thing I had ever done; that I would feel like a failure and have many sleepless nights, but to endure and persevere. Focus on the future, he urged me, and not on the challenge I felt within. He was right.

You will fail. I have, and you will as well. But we learn from it.

## PIVOT AND ACT

Uncertain times are a challenge for all of us. It's the crack-in-the-wall analogy. Faced with a challenge—the crack in the wall—those people and companies that pivot and quickly act to shore up weaknesses survive and thrive; those that don't act will falter and often fail to survive.

---

*In a crisis, go to Plan B: Be present; be kind; be helpful.*

---

One of the lessons in the RE/MAX leaders' playbook that we learned from the 2008–2010 recession is, "Talk early and often about identifying the challenges, be transparent in financial conversations with our franchisees and agents, and communicate with confidence regularly."

That's what we did in 2020.

# HOLISTIC APPROACH IS ESSENTIAL

This time around our leaders knew they had to approach the problem holistically with digital empathy top of mind. That meant conversations with clients needed to lead with genuine caring to help lessen the fear and uncertainty of COVID, the lockdown, and the future. Then conversations could turn to solving problems.

Cash flow was tight or nonexistent. But realistically, you can't ask someone how they're going to pay you and expect a reasonable answer when they're worried about putting food on the table. We had to first care about the emotions of our customers and their clients and solve this problem collectively so we could all solve the cash-flow problem together.

Unlike many real estate organizations, RE/MAX operates as a membership model. Its franchises pay a fixed fee per agent per month regardless of how much business a franchise does, plus a small percentage of commissions. That compares with other operations that generally receive a percentage of commissions as payment.

During recent tough times, among the solutions RE/MAX offered its members was deferring or waiving certain fees. The bottom line was caring about the franchisees first.

# MODEL THE RIGHT BEHAVIOR

In 2020, as CEO, I modeled the behavior to help our leaders with their client communications. I did online videos with suggestions on what we all needed to think about to help everyone through this pandemic. I also made 40 different seven-minute videos with the theme Mind, Body, Business to help people recenter their minds moving forward.

After all, if a leader is miserable and stressed, so are their employees, and they will create miserable customers. We each need to focus on our entire lives—relationships, family, nutrition, health, fitness, and spirituality. Without a balance, your wins will elude you, and your business will suffer.

We laid the right foundation, maintained the right attitude, and reaffirmed our commitment to get the job done. It wasn't a one-time action, either. Throughout the pandemic our leaders and our employees continued their holistic approach to further ensure we all came away with a win.

---

*Stalled by can't and won't? Drop those Ts now and shoot for can and won!*

---

## YOUR TURN TO FIX THINGS

In tough times, solutions to problems aren't one-dimensional; they're multifaceted. Ultimately, if you choose to embrace "I can" and be a leader, as I mentioned earlier, you do so across all of your life—not only in business, but also in health and wellness, relationships, nutrition, spirituality, and more.

We can create wins and learn from losses across all aspects of our lives. Each small win creates another small win, then another and another, and the wins snowball. Micro wins create more micro wins and add up to macro wins. This is winning by a thousand wins, one win at a time.

The wins will permeate your relationships, business and personal, and holistically build happiness and success across all pillars of your life. Sure, you will experience pauses in your wins—those are the losses (learnings). But all are a necessary recalibration on the path to more wins. Expect them, seek to overcome them, and push ahead with leading and winning. Too often we allow a loss to discourage us, and then we stop trying or become overwhelmed.

### Identifying the Problems

Do you feel or perceive stress? If the answer is "Yes," rather than shrugging it off, ask yourself, "Why?" What's the cause or causes of the stress—the crack in the wall?

If you're faced with a business challenge or trying to generate new business, the same scenario applies: What's the stressor or the challenge? What's the solution, and how can you provide it?

Author Ryan Levesque, a hugely successful online business executive, calls the approach SMIQ®, or What's The Single Most Important Question? He details his methods to generate business in his book *Ask: The Counterintuitive Online Method to Discover Exactly What Your Customers Want to Buy . . . Create a Mass of Raving Fans . . . and Take Any Business to the Next Level.*[5]

In other words, Levesque is trying to help each of us understand how we talk about our challenges. The question is, "When it comes to X, what is your greatest challenge?"

## Listen to the Language

Taking it a step further, Levesque says, when you ask a client or potential client about their greatest challenge, listen to their response and ask them to write it down using as many words as necessary. The words the client uses are the same words you need to use when dealing with that client, especially when offering a solution. Too often people in business use the business's language or jargon and not the customer's language, complicating and confusing the situation. That problem is faced throughout business and law enforcement as well. People try to use their own language as opposed to the language of the client or other person. People listen when you use their words and turn off when you use yours.

Nelson Mandela said it best when asked why he learned to speak the language of his captors while imprisoned in South Africa for so many years:

> *If you talk to a man in a language he understands, that goes to his head. If you talk to him in his own language, that goes to his heart.*[6]

---

[5]Ryan Levesque, *Ask: The Counterintuitive Online Method to Discover Exactly What Your Customers Want to Buy . . . Create a Mass of Raving Fans . . . and Take Any Business to the Next Level* (Carlsbad, CA: Hay House Business, 2019).
[6]Hathitrust, "At Home in the World: The Peace Corps Story" (University of Minnesota), vi, https://babel.hathitrust.org/cgi/pt?id=umn.31951d012241914&view=1up&seq=5.

## Learning More About You

Beyond the language used, author and friend Darren Hardy suggests that mapping our goals can help each of us develop a more balanced and focused understanding of life—and, as an extension, business.

In his book *Living Your Best Year Ever,* he suggests eight aspects of life to map:

Physical

Financial

Mental

Spiritual

Business

Lifestyle

Family

Relationships

Each has its place around a clock face. How much effort do you devote to each of these aspects of your life? Draw the face of a clock with each of the eight aspects corresponding to a number. Then, starting at the center of the clock, draw a line outward equal to the effort you devote to each aspect of life. If you invest little effort or don't have any tangible goals in an area, the line may inch out only slightly from the clock's center. Or, if you expend a great deal of time and effort on an aspect—spiritual, for example—the line may extend closer to the clock's circumference.

When you've finished your map, connect the farthest points of the lines with the goal of trying to draw a circle. This may sound complex, but it's really simple. It's an eyeopener, too, when you map your efforts and see what works and what isn't quite there in your attempt at a holistic life.

Likely there are flat spots on your life circle. Those are areas that need more work and greater investment on your part. When you work on all aspects of your life, you will find that success builds success. You will neglect certain aspects of your life at times. That's life. Just don't neglect the same part more than one day in a row. Business works the same way, too, as do your health, happiness, relationships, and overall success.

This is a concept that I've used for many years. In fact, I start each year with a new copy of Hardy's *Living Your Best Year Ever* journal. It's a great way to pay attention to your life and maintain a holistic approach. The concepts in the journal help keep you focused on all the necessary parts of your life.

## Leadership Takeaways

- Your success is up to you. Believe "I can," and you're on the way to win No. 1.
- A win isn't dollars and cents or a place or end point. It's a journey—a series of missions or experiences, and actions— that, done right, brings happiness along the way.
- A win is a set of answers to following questions:
  - What is the challenge?
  - What is the necessary attitude to get started?
  - What action or actions are necessary to overcome the challenge?
- Locus of control determines the degree to which you feel you have control over your results and ultimately your life.
- The most successful people take ownership of outcomes; they exhibit internal locus of control.
- Life is a series of missions or experiences that contribute to our playbook for life.

- Leaders model the right behavior.
- Faced with a business challenge—including generating new business—stop and think about the stressor or the challenge, then determine the solution, and how can you provide it, and then take action.
- Everyone thinks there's a secret to giving a great speech. But there's not. Approach a presentation as you would any mission or any challenge. What's the challenge? What are the solutions (your script)? Then prepare (practice), and take action (present).
- No matter the type of presentation, people want to see and hear a positive attitude, confidence, and a genuine caring.
- Uncertain times call for companies and people to pivot and act quickly to shore up any weaknesses in order to survive and thrive. Those who are slow to react, if they react at all, will falter and often fail to survive.
- Pay attention to the language you use in dealing with others. People listen when you use their words and tune out when you use yours.
- In business and in life, a holistic approach works best in the pursuit of health, happiness, relationships, and success.

# CHAPTER 2

## Our Missions Set the Playbook

*"Be strong enough to listen, wise enough to ask, and kind enough to help."*

—Adam Contos

**L**ife is a series of experiences and interactions. Each is a mission. Our actions and attitudes within these missions form our mindset and create a unique playbook for how each of us lives our lives. Companies have playbooks, too, developed and honed based on mission experiences of the company and its people.

As youngsters our imaginations take us, cardboard box and all, on that pretend mission to Mars or spur that glam and glitter dress-up doll tea party. As an adult, the late-night run to the grocery, the walk next door to help a neighbor, the early-morning meeting with your boss to avoid a personnel crisis, even the nuances of closing a hard-earned sale, all are missions that play a role in our psychological training for life.

The memories of these missions imprint our brains with responses. Like a computer search for information about something, your brain now has a situation response instead of "data not found." This is how we learn. Each time we do something, we learn from it, and we store those learnings away for future options in life.

When I first started as a contract employee at RE/MAX, I had no experience in the real estate business other than hanging out with a great lifelong friend and his mom, a very successful RE/MAX agent in the 1980s and '90s. I had spent the previous dozen years in law enforcement. But no matter where we go or what we do, there are always new opportunities and unknowns. No one is going to show us the way; it's up to each of us to draw from our previous missions and to learn and try new things. Look for those learnings. It takes effort to seek them out.

Hunger for knowledge and humility also allows us to find the opportunities and grow. No matter the business, many of the fundamentals are the same:

- Meet new people.
- Gain their trust and confidence.
- Understand their challenges.
- Help solve those challenges with kindness.

If you add "I need to sell or buy a house" to that challenge, welcome to the real estate business. And, if you're willing to learn how to do it, I also recommend finding a great leader, mentor, and teacher. That's because the barriers to entering the real estate business are low, but the barriers to success are high. Being a real estate agent isn't easy—80 to 90 percent of new agents fail in their first five years. For those who are dedicated and willing to be aggressive in their personal development, the probability of success is greater.

## THE SUM OF ALL OUR MISSIONS

The specifics of each mission are tools in your life toolbox. They're the sum of all that you have learned from your missions, and they are the framework/systems you build based on (intentional) risks you have taken. You should get excited about every mission—the last, the next, and the one after that. This is what life is about—experiences—so enjoy it.

# INTIMIDATING YET POWERFUL

Early June 1990 was the most intimidating experience of my life. It's a long story, yet an essential one because the missions associated with that experience shaped much of who I am today as a person and a leader.

It was a beautiful morning that began at the Military Entrance Processing Station in Denver. I had graduated high school the day before and was now standing in a line with a bunch of other 18-year-olds headed into the U.S. Marines. We were from all walks of life, and all in our underwear awaiting physical examinations. That may sound a bit strange, but it really wasn't much different from a bunch of teenage boys parading around a locker room. I remember the cold and the building's strange smell—that combination of mustiness and cleaning chemicals so common in old government buildings. Thus began my journey.

Fast forward to that evening. I was getting on a government bus at the San Diego airport with few personal belongings, just my wallet, a piece of paper with some addresses and phone numbers on it, a few family photos, and a folder of government documents I had accumulated throughout the day. The Marine drill instructor was herding our group of young men, yelling at us, barking orders, and hovering above us. Marine drill instructors are an amazing breed of perfection. Their uniforms are perfectly clean and ironed; their stature and physical build the epitome of athlete and warrior combined, and their stare deep and solid. Regardless of their physical height, they tower above the rest. I stand 6-foot-3 and even the drill instructors who were shorter looked down at me.

The ride from the airport was a short one to the Marine Corps Recruit Depot. The facility is perfectly maintained, and most of it is painted red and gold, the colors of the Marines, with many yellow stucco buildings with red tile rooftops surrounded by workout facilities and large blacktop drill fields. The short trip involved a lot of the drill instructors yelling at us, and a lot of us sitting at attention, hands on our laps, eyes facing forward, and answering in a loud "Yes, Sir!" to many of the questions that ended with "Do you understand?" We pulled up to one of the stucco buildings, in front of which was a series of yellow footprints painted on the ground and all lined up in a very calculated fashion. The footprints were painted in a manner that had the heels touching with the toes pointed outward, which is how you stand at attention. There are four lines of approximately 15 footprint pairs, each line representing a squad of 15 people for a total of 60, which represents a platoon size. As the bus pulled up to the building, another drill instructor got on and began yelling, walking down the aisle of the bus, telling us what was going to happen and to move fast and with intention, and by now our automatic responses were "Yes, Sir!" This was intimidating. It was supposed to be. Just like in the movies, we got off the bus, and thus the process of breaking us down and rebuilding us as U.S. Marines was underway.

Marine Corps boot camp is meant to intimidate the hell out of you. You're constantly yelled at, ordered to do pushups or other intense physical activities, and put into situations that tax you mentally and physically. Beyond the basic Marine Corps training, I took away several life lessons:

- To work for those next to you and to not let them down
- To believe in yourself and your actions
- To ignore the desire to mentally give up before your body shuts down, and to flip this paradigm—never give up as long as you are alive
- To push yourself to failure to expand your limits because you can always do more
- To know that you can be smart and strong

- To be the thinker and doer with the desire to take initiative, and not to wait for someone to tell you to move
- To believe that nothing can intimidate you

All of these principles were taught through both classroom and experiential learning. The Marine Corps instructors took you through failure, frustration, intimidation, and extreme pressures mentally and physically. They taught you and tested you, set the standards high and made you meet them all day, every day, and created an expectation of excellence. And all of these ideals were demonstrated by the Marines who were instructing you. If you ran, they ran. If you climbed, they climbed first. If you suffered in any way, they did so first.

It was true leadership by demonstration and modeling. Our leaders were tested by each other as they tested you. If you failed, so did they. The bar was very high, and results were demanded by everyone. You looked at the challenges as opportunities to show you were better than the challenge. You programmed your brain not to be intimidated, not to quit, to work for those around you, and to have very high standards. I am proud to have gone through this and feel it helped me become who I am.

## THE DOWNSIDE

I took away all this and more from Marine Corps training. Yet my training also magnified the stark and frustrating realities of the civilian world.

We live in a society where minimum effort is tolerated. At some points, we are even shamed into believing people are amazing for putting forth the minimum effort. These same people are rewarded simply for showing up and not trying. When they're pushed to perform, those pushing are labeled bullies.

First, people who want to start with a win don't wake up in the morning and ask, "What's the least I can do and still get by?" And

31

second, if someone feels bullied because an employer expects more than the minimum effort, the questions for us as leaders are:

- How do we create an environment in which people want to perform at their highest levels?
- How do we unlock someone's potential instead of pushing them to barely get by?

Those same questions apply to us as leaders, too, because we deserve what we tolerate. If we tolerate the minimum effort in ourselves, then we deserve to get the minimum effort from others.

## A PERFECT (BETTER) WORLD

Think about it. What if you wake up one morning, head to work or out to play, and suddenly everyone gives the maximum effort in everything? That's from slowing to let that other car merge onto the highway to picking up trash along the street, holding the door for another, saying "Please" and "Thank you," and cordially greeting everyone with a big smile and appreciation.

What kind of an environment would we have if all that happened—if we gave up the concept of doing only the minimum that's necessary to get by and instead aimed for the optimal best? If we moved that attitude into the workplace, how would our companies perform and what would be the customer response? This may be a dream, but what if we all try to do our best in everything and we get even 1 percent closer to that excellence? If we set our goals high, then even on mediocre days, we likely will still hit 70 percent of our capabilities or greater.

Let's all try to be better and watch our lives change. It's back to the concept of "one more" whatever to squeeze out a better product or result. We as leaders can do that without "bullying" our teams. Yes, there are people who aren't willing to go the extra mile. But as leaders we need to enthusiastically set the example.

It starts with a culture of performance and giving—give to your employees, recognize their successes, and ask others to run at that pace. Give gratitude to those who follow your example and create a culture of performance. When people see that they are rewarded to perform, better results ensue.

RE/MAX has always been a breeding ground for achievers, not tyrants. If someone who ends up in management looks down on others who don't perform, they quickly find their way out of the company. Those who see leadership as power, and don't treat others as equals, don't stay long. But those individuals who capture the enthusiasm of the team and harness it into productivity are the ones who become successful—who start with a win after win after win.

## TAKE A CHANCE

Every mission involves a series of chances—risks. Before you bristle at the thought of risk, consider that even opting to do nothing is a risk. A risk, after all, is merely a choice we make with unknown results, a gamble.

People often choose not to take a chance because they rationalize that inaction mitigates the risk and reduces the chance of a potentially negative outcome. Unfortunately, again, doing nothing is a risk. It has consequences that are unforeseeable. Exercising is a risk; so is not exercising. Driving to meet a client is a risk; so is not going. Appearing in a video to promote your product is a risk; so is not doing it.

The bottom line is that with each challenge, we must do our best to assess the problem, figure out the solutions—including the risks—and initially do all we can to minimize the negative factors before taking action. Keep in mind, though, that people who take the big chances usually end up the big winners.

## REGRET ISN'T AN OPTION

Part of being a leader is recognizing the "didn't get" versus the "did get." Dwelling on regret over a missed opportunity or deal is counterproductive. When we assign an emotional perspective to something that did or did not work, it makes a missed opportunity that much worse.

---

*Make growing and changing as natural as breathing.*

---

True leaders learn from the "didn't get" and move on. They don't dwell on a missed opportunity because to do so is a waste of energy over something that didn't happen. As with entrepreneurship, some things work out and some don't. People who dwell on the negative end up being negative. It's the crack-in-the wall analogy again. Too much negativity can collapse the wall.

When you focus on the negative, you describe yourself in terms of your shortcomings rather than your accomplishments. Both are true, but life is about striving and improving, not dwelling on what you didn't get right. Only criticizing ourselves is a dismal existence. People who can take the heat of criticism will find more successes than not. Be prepared, though: Many others will only focus on what wasn't accomplished instead of what was. Expect the heat; accept it and move on.

Keep in mind, too, that your last mission has little to do with your next mission or your overall performance. It's great to keep positive momentum going forward; just temper that positivity so you don't become complacent and expect the win every time without investing the effort.

## LEARNINGS AND LESSONS MOUNT UP

From a Cherry Hills reserve police officer, I became a full-time deputy sheriff with the Douglas County (Colorado) Sheriff's Office in 1993. Shortly after that, Douglas County became one of the fastest-growing counties in the nation. With the population growth came crime as well as opportunities to keep learning and growing—opportunities that teach valuable skills that transcend a particular job or profession. I am grateful to have learned a great deal from the amazing professionals, training officers, and leaders in the organization.

From my missions, I learned that I enjoyed the freedom of "working the street" and interacting with people, responding to in-progress calls, joining high-speed pursuits, and essentially being an integral and visible part of the community. I also learned I enjoyed helping people as well as the excitement of danger and life-and-death problem-solving. One day a cop deals with abuse and murder and the next helps a stranded expectant mother. The latter happened to me twice in one day on the job.

## EMOTIONS AND CONTROL

Problem-solving was a major part of what I did. Daily a law enforcement officer helps kids, teens, and adults learn emotional control, whether their problem is at home, in school, or in the workplace. Those experiences taught me that emotional overwhelm is a real part of life. When you learn to control your emotions, as my parents taught me, there isn't a problem you can't find the resources to solve.

So what seem on the surface to be polar opposites in terms of the jobs—cop versus CEO—really aren't at all. Rather, both present different surroundings and scenarios, but the mission lessons are much the same.

A business leader must deal with personal problems brought into the business by employees or customers. The leader has to identify the problem and understand it from a different perspective. In fact, we all carry perceived problems with us daily. It's how we and those around us deal with those problems—sometimes unknowingly—that affect how we deal with other people and shape the outcomes of our interactions.

Think about your previous jobs or professions and how you use what you learned on those missions to solve problems today.

## PAY ATTENTION TO YOUR GUT

Gut feelings are also learnings in your life playbook. Over time we hone those gut feelings with each mission we accept. Sometimes our guts help us shape impressions of people we meet; other times our guts steer us in the right direction, and sometimes, a gut feeling is a warning. It can save a business relationship or even sometimes a life.

While still a deputy sheriff, one day on the interstate I pulled over a car without license plates. I exited my cruiser, and as I walked up to the vehicle, something just didn't feel right. That silent voice—my gut—was talking to me again. As I approached the car's door, the driver tried to push it open. I asked him to stay in the car, but he looked hard at me and tried to shoulder the door open anyway. I blocked it. The look on his face told me something was off, so I ordered him to put his hands on the steering wheel. Then I noticed his wife beside him and two small kids in the backseat.

"What's going on?" I asked. By now my gut was raging silently. He stared at me intently and quietly told me he didn't want his wife or kids to see this. I asked for his license and registration. He offered the license, but the registration, he said, was in the glovebox and we could talk about it behind the car. "Please get the registration," I said. He reached over with his right hand to get the registration while at the same time moving his left hand behind him. That's when I saw the gun.

This had the potential to become a very bad situation, one that could balloon quickly out of control. And it's a situation that most civilians have no idea how to deal with quietly and safely. A man is trying to reach for a gun and to separate you from his car, kids, and wife so "they won't see this" along the side of the highway. It's not a time to jump to a conclusion, but instead to be confident and articulate and to act immediately. That's what we train for as law enforcement.

"Stop immediately, do not move," I said very directly. "I see the gun. You won't win this." Then I radioed my partner and carefully controlled the situation until my partner arrived. This potentially volatile interaction was quickly and quietly resolved without incident.

Had I not heeded my gut warning that something was wrong, I could have ended up being shot by the side of the road. Instead, the situation went from potential chaos to controlled calm.

## INSTINCTS MATTER

Whatever, the situation, we need to listen to our instincts. If something doesn't seem right, if you feel like something is wrong, or your gut gets uneasy or tight, that's a sign. Your natural survival instincts are kicking in and sending you a message. Our survival instinct allows us to subconsciously notice noises and movement or, when speaking with someone, to sense deception or subterfuge.

At the very least, it's a signal to pause and reassess the situation.

Especially as a leader, don't ignore what doesn't feel right, whether it's related to ethics, operations, budgets, personnel, or any other facet of your business. When your gut starts screaming at you, change your perspective. Ask questions, look around, adjust your actions, and see what happens. Doing nothing is what gets you in trouble.

Of course, decisions should be benchmarked against data, but pay attention to gut feelings. I've begun potential transactions that seem like great ideas and a perfect fit, only to turn around and walk away later because they "felt" really bad. I remember one particular case where the other party's true intentions became apparent as we went deeper into the transaction, and they had little to do with the stated goal of a collective win for all of us. If I hadn't listened to my gut, the deal could have led to negative repercussions for our company.

## CRUCIAL INPUT

In life, ignoring your gut can do more than simply thwart a business deal. I know that firsthand from years on the streets as a cop and on SWAT calls. Those "something isn't right" thoughts that you can't quite figure out mean something. At the very least, they tell you to relocate your perspective and look again or take action and discover something.

While traveling, my gut feelings have helped keep my family and me safe, too. One evening my wife and I were walking down a street in Quebec City, Canada. It was late and dark, but there were other people out on the streets so I wasn't too worried about our safety. Then my gut kicked in.

We had to walk down a stretch of sidewalk sandwiched between a long hedge and a busy street. I looked ahead about 100 feet in front of us and saw a group of four young men standing together. They looked hard at us and then quickly began talking and appeared to agree on something. Two of the men took off running along the other side of the tall hedge. as the other two began walking slowly toward us. I knew what was happening. They were encircling us so we would be trapped.

I always carry a small flashlight for personal defense purposes. Light at night is a powerful tool against potential criminals and makes a great defensive weapon as well. I turned on the light, told my wife to stay close to me, and began walking hard into the storm. This caught the attention of the two approaching from the front. They saw the bison heading into the storm and decided they would rather go the other way and did so quickly.

I swung around to face the other two young men, light on, and with serious intent. They rounded the corner to head our way, saw me, and put on the brakes. They also decided it wasn't worth their effort.

Had I not noticed the tiny indicators of others' intentions in this situation, we likely would have been mugged or worse. We didn't wait to see what else was going to happen, but I'm sure they didn't want to wish us a wonderful evening and to hang out.

My gut also has steered me away from bad businesspeople and deals. Instead of listening to the too-good-to-be-true stories, I've said no up front.

The bottom line is that you must read the people and situations around you, pay attention to your gut feelings that point to the micro actions of others, and encourage your teams to do so as well, and share those feelings with others.

## TALKING POINTS

My many missions working in law enforcement also taught me the power of words and attitude. Respect opens doors, as does gratitude, whether you are a cop interviewing someone regarding a crime or a sales agent talking to a potential client. Often initially you get push-back, disrespected, or turned down, but you nonetheless must keep trying with kindness, respect, and professionalism. Have endurance, too. When you lead with a smile, gratitude, and respect, you are in a better position to set yourself up for a win.

For example, instead of responding "OK" to someone, try the words "I respect that" when it comes to an opinion, an idea, or a statement. "I respect what you're saying," for example. Or say, "Thank you," when someone shares their feelings in an emotional situation. Most of all, truly mean what you say. Give gratitude and it will be returned at some point.

As I discussed in the last chapter, word choice makes a difference, as does attitude.

## FAILURES ARE WINS, TOO

We all fail at some missions—that's unavoidable. The great wisdom of fails, though, is what we learn from them. The takeaway turns the negative outcome into a positive—a win. With a loss, ask yourself, "But what did I learn from that? What is my takeaway? What will I do differently next time?"

People on the path to success don't see failures; they see learning opportunities. They embrace failure because when they break something, they learn why or how and move forward. They also know that plans don't always work, but the planning process is an integral part of what makes things work because planning is as much about finding ways that something won't work as it is finding the way that it will work.

These individuals also realize that successes or fails are both part of the process of creating options to find success. They recognize that there is always more than one way and there *is* always a way. After all, the light bulb we take for granted today was the culmination of a thousand failures before success.

---

*"I didn't fail 1,000 times. The light bulb was an invention with 1,000 steps."*

—Thomas Edison on the supposed 1,000 failed attempts to make a working light bulb

---

Think of losses as learnings and failures as finders; they're both great opportunities to become smarter and better at what you do.

## TOUGH TIMES

At the frontend of the 2008 recession, RE/MAX founder Dave Liniger shared the following wise thoughts on tough times:

*The lesson is, will you quit? And if you don't, what will you have learned when we come out of this problem? Because we will come out of it eventually.*

The Great Recession of 2008–2010 was among the most challenging years for RE/MAX as it was for many companies. The housing sector reeled, and industries and companies collapsed. Alongside our partners in the business, RE/MAX struggled to make it through.

But as Dave had predicted, we survived the recession because challenges are opportunities. Extreme difficulties give birth to new concepts and ideas. The Great Recession taught the real estate industry the challenges of subprime lending. It also reinforced the importance of treating everyone with kindness and respect, especially during difficult times, because someday you may do business with them when the tables are turned.

Dave has another great forward-looking confidence statement for challenging times: "*This too shall pass*." Countless people have repeated those words throughout history because they are powerful coming from a leader. Your teams and your people don't have to know when they will get through the challenge, only that you have the confidence in their abilities to get to the other side of the problem.

## RELATIONSHIPS MAKE THE DIFFERENCE

Relationships and the support they offer are essential in challenging times. Faced with a tough situation, leaders initially step back and consider the risks, the opportunities, and their supporters. Every challenge involves people who are afraid as well as those who have confidence in their leaders and will stand by them. The latter—the result of cultivated strong relationships—not only magnify a leader's message to others who are crippled by fear but also reinforce a leader's motivation to find solutions to the challenge.

Most people who faced foreclosure during the recession bought their homes during the housing market boom. These new homeowners needed a trusted advisor to understand their predicament and help them solve their problems. The real estate agents who had maintained relationships with those homeowners and cared about them guided them through some difficult solutions, including short sales and foreclosures that had to occur to correct the market.

During the recession and the more recent pandemic, I regularly met with groups of franchisees and agents to talk about the challenges and how to overcome them. Afterwards, I always reached out to several individuals in attendance with whom I had strong relationships. I wanted feedback on whether I had delivered the right message. I also always asked for their advice and help. Too few leaders do this because they are afraid to share humility for fear of appearing weak (more on the importance of humility in Chapter 8).

## THE ROLE OF EMOTIONS

No one can predict the future challenges each of us will face; what is predictable, though, is how people will respond and how they will consciously deploy their emotions—whether kindness and compassion or frustration and anger. Establishing caring relationships helps ensure the former rather than the latter prevails.

How will you react in your missions when a situation deteriorates? Your challenges are your choices and your opportunities, so choose wisely.

## DEBRIEFING IS ESSENTIAL

With a SWAT team, there's a debrief after any mission or challenge. In business, there should be a postmortem, too, to look back at lessons learned during a project. That look back helps us understand and avoid making the same mistake again and we grow in the process.

The reality is that during every mission, project, or challenge, there will be something that in hindsight should have been done differently. Recognizing that is essential to improvement. Unfortunately, most people don't take the time as a team to share postmortem thoughts. Instead, they end up with only their view of what went down, and often their view is dominated by the emotional frustration from parts of a mission that didn't succeed. "Glad that's over with" is the usual line of thinking. What these people don't realize is that many other aspects of the mission went well. They don't want to discuss it, though, at the risk of others noticing they might have done something wrong.

Team postmortems that review the victories as well as the shortcomings maximize the lessons learned from a mission. Even if it was a solo mission, "What did I learn?" is the most valuable approach.

Often businesses that do look back make the mistake of not doing a deep enough look-back for it to be truly effective. Their process instead is general and simplified—what went well and what didn't.

Here's a simple four-step lookback process that can apply to any mission in work or life:

1. Celebrations: What went well? List everything, step by step, that was effective and efficient.

2. Frustrations: What didn't go well? List everything that was inefficient, painful, or challenging. Be honest.

3. Eliminations: Where was money, time, or effort wasted? What could have been done differently? What caused other problems? (Your answers here should delve more deeply into the challenges than in steps 1 and 2.) Your answers in turn can help you identify scalability and leverage possibilities.

4. Deviations: What other options could have been used? In other words, how might we complete the mission next time? Plan the mission again from the beginning. Ask why, how, and what if. Remember, you don't know what you don't know, so explore.

As an added step, consider the people in the mission. Would the mission have worked better with people in different assignments or with different people? It's not about ego; it's about accomplishment. When everyone wins in a mission, everyone wins as a team, and that should be the goal.

## LESSONS FROM ENTREPRENEURSHIP

Entrepreneurs understand the importance of debriefing because they are often on their own, take the biggest chances, and score some of the biggest wins. But entrepreneurship is tough; the failures outnumber the successes. I learned that firsthand. As business coaches and books oft repeat, though, it's not about stopping when you fail. Entrepreneurship takes grit and understanding that nothing is going to be easy, but nothing is impossible.

We need to go back to the tenets of leadership—assess the problem, find the solution, take action, and move forward for the win. Essential to the process, however, is to not stop taking action. Things may not work out, but there's always next time. When you quit is when you fail. Consistent effort through failures leads to success.

## BUILDING YOUR BUSINESS

Building a business isn't complicated. It's not easy, either. The simple part is building the framework; the hard part is executing on that framework. As with anything else in life that leads to success, a business takes effort. That effort is relentless, consistent, and focused every day, even in the face of seemingly repeated failure.

I built my security consulting business based on what I knew I wanted to do—to provide a great service to help others. The big challenge, though, was how to get others to buy my services, especially when theoretically they could come up with the ideas themselves.

I started with a simple plan that among other things addressed:

- How to build a customer base
- How to get people interested in my solutions to their challenges
- How to keep in touch with those people thereby building relationships with them

To accomplish all this, I started by building relationships. I spoke with individuals and companies and shared anecdotal stories, surveys, and conversations with businesses, as well as my learnings from research on personal and corporate safety and my law enforcement perspective. When people began to listen, I arranged one-on-one meetings with people and companies to personalize my philosophies to their business and challenges. Once I accomplished that, I was able to price the product and reach an agreement with them. It was a smooth process but revolved around relationships first. People don't care what you know until they know you care.

## REAL ESTATE GRIT

Real estate agents are among the grittiest entrepreneurs I've ever met. They are 100 percent commission-based and willing to speak to unlimited numbers of people to find a customer. That attitude compares with many others in sales who sit and wait for the customer to come to them.

Agents who are successful scale their presence by building a network of people who find business for them. They maintain relationships with those people, and that magnifies an agent's presence because the network spreads the word.

You've heard people say, "I'm not the smartest one in the room but I'm the hardest worker." Sure, the hardest worker will surpass the most intelligent. But we all have the opportunity both to work hard and to learn so that we can become the smartest, hardest workers. That combo truly makes magic.

## CONSISTENCY WINS

That's another lesson I learned as an entrepreneur. As the ancient Greek philosopher Aristotle reportedly said, "We are what we repeatedly do. Excellence, then, is not an act, but a habit." Very wise words. Consistency of action and attitude in business and in life will net results, build amazing relationships, and provide the wins.

In business and in life, whatever you do, you should do it enough to see consistent results. Doing something only once and then abandoning it because you don't think it works isn't enough. It simply means that you haven't done whatever it is long enough or with enough repetition to determine whether it works.

If you look at the top performers in real estate, they're not doing something exciting every day; they are doing something consistent every day. They're not chasing the distractions in the industry, either. They are simply doing what they know works.

Picture this: You get to your workstation—whether it's a Starbucks or an actual office—first thing in the morning. You know you must contact a minimum of 20 customers that day. Typically, most people would consider that a monotonous task with a significant amount of failure built into those potential customer interactions. But those individuals who succeed at customer interaction and follow-up get excited about the prospect of making 20 telephone calls. They approach the challenge as a game, not a burden, and they are out to win that game. They want to discover if it's possible to garner even one more of whatever they're doing or pitching or selling because one more in a monotonous environment is incredibly powerful. That's whether it's doing one more pushup, running one more lap, or making one more telephone call to create one more customer.

The reality of the monotony of business, as in any other part of life, is that "one more" is often many times more powerful than "I almost did it." Many people think "close" is good enough, whereas those who believe in one more are the ones who set the records. The magic lies in the repetitions you do when everyone else has quit for the day. Your one more adds up to hundreds more annually. And that's what the person walking across the stage to pick up the biggest trophy at the sales conference is doing—one more.

## ATTITUDE AND MORE RELATIONSHIPS

The most successful entrepreneurs are leaders who value relationships. They know that being an entrepreneur means being an amazing human and cultivating all the relationships you have the privilege to create while helping those people solve their challenges with your product or service.

Entrepreneurs are helpers, not sellers. Selling happens, but only because people want you to help them with the transaction because they know you're the best person for it. Too often sales teaches us, "You must be a closer." Not so. I don't want to be closed; I want to be helped.

Yes, you have to close the deal in a transaction. But make it a result of the relationship, not the termination of a process. Closings are exciting in business, especially in real estate. They're a celebration that signifies helping another person. I see a closing not as the end, but as the beginning of a lifelong relationship of helping each other.

Unique to entrepreneurs, too, is that they open their eyes every day with an energy unknown to everyone else. They have the "I get to" mindset rather than the "I have to" mindset. That's why they can cope with the overwhelming challenges of running a business. They get to do it. They don't have to go to work; they get to go make a difference in life with their efforts. It's an exciting mindset to have.

# KNOWING WHEN TO STOP

Among my various part-time entrepreneurial adventures while still a full-time cop was an online law enforcement supply company that sold products to officers and government organizations. Perhaps the choice of businesses wasn't the best for the 1990s, when people were still leery of online sales. But I always dreamed of owning my own business and liked to nurture customer experiences and service, so I tried it.

The venture was slightly profitable, and I enjoyed being able to serve many of my friends and colleagues. That was the upside; the downside was maintaining inventory, shipping, supply chain management, and all that goes along with selling products. Wisely, after a couple of years, I realized that I belonged in a more service-based business and opted to close the company. The online business taught me a lot, though, which I rolled over into my next business.

# A WORD ABOUT SUCCESS

Success isn't as much a destination as it is part of an ongoing journey, a direction and effort made up of a series of missions. With each win, we hunger for more.

Every now and then, you change directions as part of readjusting your efforts to continue to create success. Individuals on the success journey know the future, not the past, holds growth, so they don't look back except to learn and remember. The past provides the missions and the lessons—some painful and others not so. But they all serve a purpose to help each of us grow and become better.

When individuals relive their past and dwell on it, they fail to grow. The secret to learning more is to live more.

# YOUR TOOLBOX FOR THE JOURNEY

Whether someone is an entrepreneur, an officer in a major corporation, or an employee opting to win every day, we all need tools to help us on the journey to winning in business and in life. These tools are the guidance, lessons, and experiences of others that can help us transform our own lives for the better.

A car mechanic, after all, doesn't use just one tool to repair a vehicle. They have multiple tools and devices to identify and solve the problems. The same is true when it comes to fixing our lives and our businesses.

In the following pages, you'll learn more about the tools you need to start with a win. Among those tools:

- Learn to overcome your emotions and take action.
- Leaders are lifelong learners.
- Always share your learnings with others.
- Build your action plans, and guide others to solve challenges.
- Be present and passionate about your people and your work.

- Lose the ego and learn to embrace vulnerability.
- Don't be afraid to reach out to others for guidance and help.
- Take time to celebrate the wins.

## Leadership Takeaways

- The secret to learning more is to live more.
- The great wisdom of fails is what we learn from them. The takeaway turns the negative outcome into a positive—a win.
- Debriefings are essential, even in a solo mission. Team postmortems that review the victories as well as the short-comings maximize the lessons learned from a mission.
- Follow the four-step look-back process:
  - Celebrations: What went well? List everything, step by step, that was effective and efficient.
  - Frustrations: What didn't go well? List everything that was inefficient, painful, or challenging. And be honest.
  - Eliminations: Where was money, time, or effort wasted? What could have been done differently? What caused other problems? (Delve more deeply into the challenges. Your answers in turn can help you identify scalability and leverage possibilities.)
  - Deviations: What other options could have been used? In other words, how might we complete the mission next time? Plan the mission again from the beginning. Ask why, how, and what if, too. Remember, you don't know what you don't know, so explore.

- Consider the people in the mission. Would the mission have worked better with people in different assignments or with different people? It's not about ego; it's about accomplishment.

- Entrepreneurship is not about stopping when you fail. It's not about ego, either. It's about accomplishment.

- When faced with a challenge revert to the tenets of leadership—assess the problem, find the solution, take action, and move forward for the win. Essential to the process, however, is not to stop taking action.

# PART II

# YOUR TOOLBOX

# CHAPTER 3

# Party With the Beast (Your Emotions)

*"Moments of fear and doubt have value; they put you in a stronger place."*

—Adam Contos

**W**e all live with the Beast.

Inside each of us lurks this creature called the Beast—our emotions, its form personal and unique to our minds and actions. The Beast dominates us through fear and self-doubt and threatens to overshadow all that we do. It can be our greatest source of avoidance or our greatest lever for success if we learn to harness its incredible power.

Your Beast is wondering if you can accomplish something or if you will survive your challenges. It's other people's opinions, and it is success or not at work. Ultimately, the Beast is your biggest competitor.

Leaders deal with the Beast every day. People invariably ask what our biggest competition is. The answer is to reflect on all that's in this book as well as to understand that each of us has the Beast within. And each of us does battle with our own fear, doubt, and overwhelm.

## FRIEND OR FOE?

As a child, my Beast was a giant creature with bulging muscles, piercing eyes, and bad intentions. I would close my eyes and see it. The Beast haunted me in the darkness of my closet or under the bed at night. It was a noise I couldn't place, a shadow I couldn't name, the unknown.

## FEAR ISN'T UNIQUE

Rather than chuckle at the imagination of a child, think about your own monsters. We all face similar fears—beasts—throughout our lives. Perhaps your Beast hovers over your shoulder when you take a test, apply for a job, cold call a potential client, or speak to a colleague.

Unless each of us learns to understand this fictitious character that surfaces regularly, it will continue to haunt us all our lives, becoming smarter, stronger, and more capable, and stymieing our hopes of reaching our true potential.

## MAJOR FORCE

Our emotions determine the decisions we make. Too often we're so busy trying to identify where we are emotionally that we're paralyzed into inaction. I call that analysis paralysis.

Scientists have identified as few as six and up to more than two dozen human emotions. The six are happiness, sadness, anger, surprise, fear, and disgust.[1] However, even a half-dozen emotions are too many emotional classifications to sort out in the chaos of life. I prefer to approach the taming of the Beast in terms of two distilled, easily identifiable and understandable emotions—fear and love. With fewer options, it's easier to make decisions and act even during the most chaotic situation.

---

[1]Jasmine Anwar, "How Many Different Human Emotions Are There?" *Greater Good,* September 8, 2017, https://greatergood.berkeley.edu/article/item/how_many_different_human_emotions_are_there.

# TAMING THE BEAST

Years ago, a fellow SWAT commander from another team, Bruce, taught me how to cope with the Beast. Bruce is an amazing person, a warrior, and servant leader. He's also a very purposeful, caring, and calm leader with confidence that resonates with everyone around him.

We were briefing for a complex SWAT operation. Bruce knew some of the officers were worried and overwhelmed by the circumstances—read that as afraid—but he also knew we all were capable of safely and successfully accomplishing the mission. So he shared with everyone how to tame the Beast within:

*The Beast is inside all of us. It's self-doubt, fear, and the unknown on the other side of the door of the building you're about to breach under gunfire. It's doubt about your ability to take action, doubt about your knowledge, training, and preparation; doubt about your teamwork and collaboration with your fellow warriors.*

*All these doubts cause hesitation and lack of focus. They reduce your precision and cause you to miss your mark when you must perform.*

*This fear, doubt, and overwhelm is your Beast. It lives in each of us and is our desire to be the best but wondering if we will fall short—all of which causes us to fall short. It is yourself asking yourself, "Have you done your very best?"*

*Your Beast can win if you let it. It can create internal fear and overwhelm that prevents you from being at your best. But your Beast may also be your best friend, your leverage to perform better, to be more focused, and precise. Your Beast can be your greatest ally in accomplishing your tasks, goals, and missions in life.*

*The choice is yours to make right now. You must decide how to handle your Beast. You can go through that door and fight your hardest. Or you can be distracted and overwhelmed by the Beast and allow it to take your attention, slow you down, and make you less than you know you are. You can go into the fight and enjoy your time with your Beast; embrace it and allow it to help you understand how great you have become.*

*You party with your Beast, and it will be there to support your efforts to be your very best. You just need to tell your Beast whether you want it to make you better or make you worse. How do you want to party with the Beast?*

## Beast in Business

The same principles apply when the Beast surfaces in a typical business scenario, which it does daily as a lost deal or an upset client. The foundation for its appearance is absolutely the same as the noise in your closet as a kid. The Beast shows up as the unknown—perhaps a statement from a client, a social media post, a rumor about a deal, or simply you playing the what-if game in your head over an interaction with a client.

# TAKE ACTION

In the face of your own fear, take action. If it's a business deal, exercise the relationship with the client. Call them and talk about whatever; ask them how they're doing and be there to help that person with whatever challenges arise. Building these types of one-on-one relationships is extremely effective, especially during economic downturns. Rather than simply doing a one-time business transaction with a client, you have an ongoing friendship. You know where you stand with that person; the relationship is reinforced, and the Beast disappears.

Do you remember the first time you made a presentation before your boss, or worse, your board of directors? Did you try to avoid it? Maybe you overwhelmed yourself and got "sick."

# OVERCOME THE FEAR

The first time I had to present in front of our board of directors was rough. It was early in my career at RE/MAX and just the makeup of our board would intimidate anyone. It included business superstars like private equity leaders, CEOs of major companies, war veterans, and an amazing leader who had flown the space shuttle several times.

I was worried even contemplating my presentation. What would they think of me? Afterwards, would they tell my boss, "Fire that guy?" Or would they say, "Wow, that was really valuable information."

I prepared and prepared because preparation reduces stress if it helps you get closer to being comfortable and confident. Preparation keeps the Beast at bay by creating automatic actions and gives you the ability to turn emotions into actions. Before the meeting I spent some time with my Beast and decided that I knew what I needed to get the presentation done, and I did it.

Since that initial challenge, I speak and present to our board regularly and make big business decisions that initially would have paralyzed me. But now I know better how to party with the Beast. And I understand that no matter the amount of rationalizing, there really is only one way to party with the Beast—take action.

# FACE IT HEAD ON

Your Beast could just as easily rear its nasty presence when it's time to talk to the boss about a pay raise or to take on more responsibility. I know one outstanding agent who faces the Beast whenever he meets a client for the first time. He has completed hundreds of transactions successfully but still has self-doubt when explaining his value to others. His Beast surfaces when it's time to win business, yet he has learned how to party with the Beast.

Whatever the situation, we often avoid opportunity because of the unknown and the discomfort—the Beast—associated with it. Avoidant people seek the comfort of knowing results, outcomes, and answers before acting or taking a risk. They do so with a false sense of security, believing that knowing the outcome ahead of time somehow reduces the risk. The reality is that no one knows the real results of doing something until someone actually tries to do it. Don't try to avoid the Beast, or it will sneak up on you. Allow the Beast's presence, but make sure it knows its place.

Leaders like my agent friend above have learned to face the Beast and come away with a win. We can't fight the Beast, but we can embrace it and harness its strengths to create focus and confidence.

# SELF-DOUBTS

Harnessing self-doubt is among the greatest strengths we have. Allowing fear to rule our lives is the greatest weakness.

Psychologists sometimes refer to the self-doubt some people experience as imposter syndrome or the imposter phenomenon. Studies over time have demonstrated that up to 70 percent of society experience this self-doubt in their lives and are afraid of being "found out" as a fraud.[2]

However, this is a cycle in which we ultimately either procrastinate or overprepare for achievement-related tasks or assignments. Either choice reinforces our belief that we succeed because we are lucky or because we reduce our risk of failure by being overly prepared.

The reality is that our Beast is nothing more than a quality-control mechanism to ensure that we focus on being the best we can be. It's not designed to prevent us from taking action, and it certainly isn't intended to convince us that we are frauds.

In fact, Grammy-winning author Maya Angelou once said that she thought she would be found out as a fraud after writing each of her 11 amazing books. The reality is that she isn't a fraud but a generous soul who shares the self-doubt we all experience.

Once at an exclusive mastermind of 100 successful business leaders, our host Darren Hardy asked the audience of entrepreneurs and high performers if anyone felt like an imposter. Nearly everyone in the room raised their hands.

Hardy went on to describe how anyone who achieves anything has doubts. As leaders we choose not to follow the herd, which is an act of independence bound to create doubt. We are determined to perform better every day, but we're not sure we have the talent or

---

[2]P.R. Clance and S.A. Imes, "The Imposter Phenomenon in High Achieving Women: Dynamics and Therapeutic Intervention," *Psychotherapy: Theory, Research, and Practice* 15 (no. 3, Fall 1978).

the ability. As a result, psychologically each of us incurs the risk of imposter syndrome.

But we all can defeat the fear, the Beast within. We can deconstruct and defeat it with our conscious actions. Let's examine some of the emotions we all face and how we can deconstruct and tame them.

# FEAR: THE DEFAULT EMOTION

A threat is simply a situation with unknown consequences. But as humans we're genetically programmed to default to fear in the face of a threat, real or imagined. It's the fight-or-flight response with a freeze option ingrained in human beings since prehistoric times.

## The Survival Instinct

Faced with a threat, our brains revert to the survival instinct. Today that means we observe or envision the problem or danger, then, based on our playbook—including imagination, movies, experiences, and other rationalizations—we determine a course of action. Unfortunately, these scenarios don't solve a problem. Rather, they magnify our emotions and prompt blame and excuses as to why we can't or shouldn't face our threat and take action.

Overwhelm takes over, compounding the problem. Anger and frustration enter into the equation, too. Nothing results but more fear and more anger. Typically, productivity stops and nothing gets accomplished. The person operating out of fear thinks they are doing something—saving themselves—but in reality, they're setting themselves up for the failure they fear.

In the wild, the fight-or-flight response was designed to help keep humans alive. Today, this fear response is more complex as it steers our social behaviors, relationships, careers, interactions, and more.

I'm reminded of a Japanese proverb: "Fear is only as deep as the mind allows." That's right; you decide whether fear controls you and your actions or not.

## Defeat It

Fear can be deconstructed and defeated. It's actually a pretty simple process that most of us have been doing all our lives.

As a little kid, we may have stood at the foot of a diving board or on the platform, or at the bottom of a ladder trying to summon the courage to act. We were afraid, but even if it took one or two or 22 times of backing down, we finally went for it. We took action. Fear is a natural deterrent; action is what tames the Beast.

## Valuable Tool

One of the most powerful tools a leader—especially someone in sales—can have is the ability to recognize the fear response in others. Overwhelm is a fear response; so are excuses and redirection of attention or blame. When people respond out of fear, their work suffers. Either they don't get their work done or they do it poorly.

Why does all this discussion about fear response matter in business? Simple: Humans are extremely intelligent beings, and, with the right amount of confidence and effort, they can accomplish nearly anything if they keep the fear response out of their emotions. That's one reason why sales is so difficult for many people and why they try to avoid it. But those of us who face the Beast and ignore the fear make great salespeople.

In business, we must teach ourselves to mostly ignore our innate fear response—the fight-or-flight response of our ancestors—and understand that people can't eat you when you try to sell a product or pitch an idea. All they can do is say no (more on that later).

# THE OPPOSITE OF FEAR: LOVE

Love is unconditional giving, a positive attitude, and optimism. It's connection. Love doesn't take a great situation, just a great attitude. Love diffuses fear, too, and that can work in your favor, especially in business. During my years in law enforcement, I was in some absolutely horrible situations that prompted fear of physical harm and even death. In the very worst of those situations, my colleagues and I would crack a joke or say something nice about each other out of love. The thought would overshadow the potential fear and kept us focused on the job at hand.

The next time someone begins to rationalize, argue, complain, or display some other manifestation of fear, try deploying love. It makes all the difference, and you'll start with a win.

# THE RISK

Love also is a willingness to take a risk because giving is a risk. Will the recipient decline the offer, gift, or effort? That rejection can be overwhelming. For example, if you offer a client something of value, you risk being told no, "not interested," or being pushed away. Yet you still try. If you were afraid, you wouldn't bother to reach out. You would stay "safe" within your shell. That's why people who are afraid make lousy sales agents.

Love is an unconditional willingness to help others and to accept their rejection with gratitude, not attitude. The same dynamics are at play when an apology would make everything better. Apologizing is one of the greatest forms of vulnerable giving, yet so many people are afraid to apologize. Often, we blame ego and the inability to admit that we were wrong, but fundamentally it's a lack of love, which is fear. The fear is that someone will think less of us or the fear of being perceived as transparent or weak. The reality of an apology is that it's worth much more than you can imagine, and costs nothing but ego. We shouldn't be afraid to use it.

# TRUE LEADERSHIP

Love overcomes the fear. When someone approaches another person with love, that person has true leadership potential. They are willing to approach a situation, yield to it, and harness the mutual energy of the participants.

These also are people who inspire others. They gather their love and confidence through their connections with others and in turn focus the energy on actions. Such individuals are clear in their communication and transparent with their feelings and the situation. They care about the emotions of those receiving their message and recognize that the recipient is likely in fear mode.

---

*"The two things you cannot give yourself are personal attention and appreciation."*

—Dale Carnegie (1937)

---

## More Wisdom

Dale Carnegie, the great self-help guru and author, wrote decades ago that one of the greatest gifts we can give with love is sincere appreciation.[3] He wasn't talking about flattery, which is appreciation without sincerity and is self-serving to the giver. Appreciation with sincerity reflects that someone cares and is willing to give love.

Personal attention is another way that leaders share love and diffuse fear. Try a simple smile and kind words like "I love coming into your store" or "I love your passion for this." That kind of personal attention and acknowledgment is important in life and especially in business when it comes to developing relationships and starting with a win.

Even "How are you today?" can actually be a game changer. All of these small efforts, including a simple smile, reflect gratitude, kindness, and appreciation.

Recently my daughter, Ashleigh, and I were at the drive-through window of a coffee shop. Ashleigh told the cashier that she loved her makeup and that changed the relationship between my daughter and this cashier. They exchanged smiles, and though we asked for

---

[3]Dale Carnegie, *How to Win Friends and Influence People* (New York: Simon & Schuster, 2010).

nothing, the cashier would have done practically anything to help us have the best experience possible at the coffee shop.

## Magical Words

Appreciation is magic. It may seem gratuitous to say things like "Thanks for all you do" or "I appreciate your hard work, thank you," but those little gestures go a long way toward building positive relationships and morale.

These words go even further if a supervisor or coworker is present. When a company leader makes these kinds of comments publicly for others to hear, it's powerful reinforcement of a positive company culture.

As the CEO of RE/MAX I make it a point to compliment employees to their supervisors. Giving the compliments is satisfying to me, the giver, and is incredibly impactful to the recipient. Those words go a long way when it comes to employee motivation and retention, too.

Yet public compliments are one of the most overlooked aspects of leadership. Simple attention and praise change how employees view a company. A boss who cares is often better than an extra day off or some small perk.

Here's an experiment to try. Pick a couple of hours or even a day, and smile at everyone you walk past or meet. You'll be surprised at how good you feel and how good you make others feel, too. Or try this: When you're in a group setting—even virtually—pick out an accomplishment or "shout-out" that you can give someone in the room. It's amazing how recognizing one person's efforts, an anniversary in the company, or even their kids playing a sport can change the environment.

# IDENTIFYING LOVE AND FEAR

The ability to recognize emotions like love and fear is a valuable asset for a leader or anyone involved in business interactions or sales.

You can hone your ability by paying close attention to the responses of people with whom you interact. Write down their responses and think about them.

A few questions to consider:

- How did they react? What words did they use? What body language?
- What action or emotion triggered their response?
- Why do you think they reacted that way?

Also, when you're in a meeting (even a virtual one), out in public, or at work, observe how others act when confronted with a challenge or an opportunity. Again, write down their responses, think about them, and ask yourself why they reacted that way. Did they rationalize why they are unable to do something? Did they make an excuse (and could their behavior be rooted in fear—the flight scenario)? Did they defer the decision? (Again, perhaps the flight scenario.) Or did they simply not answer or turn away (that is, freeze from fear)?

If you try this enough, you'll learn to recognize the fear/love response in those with whom you interact. That's an important skill to help defuse issues and solve problems.

## Confrontation

Have you ever noticed that when someone is upset about something and you confront them with something else, that often sets them off? That's meeting fear with fear, and all it does is magnify the fear response. Or if they freeze and you freeze too, they become more fearful.

The only way to deal with someone in a fear moment is to deploy love. If someone starts to rationalize, argue, complain, or whatever, confront them with love, seriously. You'll be surprised at how powerful that act can be coming from a leader. Remember Carnegie's two items we cannot give ourselves: personal attention and appreciation. Give one of those to whoever needs it, be sincere, and watch what happens.

## Emotionally Bankrupt

Have you ever been around someone who is on the attack, reacting negatively to everything, yelling, belittling, and insulting? These people are so enraged they can't even stop themselves to help others understand the situation or challenge. There is no legitimate discussion or constructive feedback. There is only a polarized one-track mind bent on attack—whether the target is a business or a person or even a situation or a deal. This is emotional bankruptcy.

Most situations can be explained, and people may agree to disagree, but the important part is the agreeing. Agreement happens with respect and understanding. People are emotionally bankrupt when they resort to name-calling and insults or to degrading others by judging their education level, personal perspective and choices, or heritage.

Instead, what if we said, "Maybe that person or group sees what I see from a different perspective. Maybe I should find out what that perspective is. They don't have to agree with my perspective, but I need to respect the fact that they can think differently than I do."

While you may think I'm referring to events in the news, I'm not. This is strictly business. Would you sell your business idea to someone who is bankrupt? Don't sell your emotions to that person, either.

A major challenge in business is that some people who resort to emotional bankruptcy are very good at sales. They come to a meeting and sell the emotion of their situation. Others may use their emotions as weapons—they bully and push for answers and solutions. They may be good at it and influence strongly, and so they end up winning. They use these tactics again and again. That doesn't make it the right way to conduct business or life.

You may not always have the right answers with everything you do. But if you act with integrity in whatever you pursue and work in your people's best interests, you can fail and learn. You can make it through difficulties. People respect your ability not to succeed in everything, and they don't fault you personally for less-than-successful outcomes.

Here's another tough situation that involves people who are emotionally bankrupt. You're a leader in an emotionally charged situation. A gang is forming against you—we'll call them the "pissed-off club." Often they don't really know why they are so angry, so there's no answer to give as a leader. Or the group is so mad, even if a leader provides sound answers, they don't listen. The bottom line as a leader is that you listen, you suck it up, and you go on. This too is part of being a leader.

---

*Never meet fear with fear; always use love.*

---

# OVERWHELM

The dictionary defines overwhelm as "defeat completely." That's not a slight setback or a partial defeat; it's total deflation, complete and utter collapse. Overwhelm also is one of the most powerful emotions hiding in the Beast inside all of us.

## Point of No Return

Consider how overwhelm happens in a practical sense. The SWAT world operates with the objective to surprise adversaries, overwhelm them, and take command of the situation quickly and with the fewest possible injuries or problems. The team knows what it needs to do, has a solid and rehearsed plan with contingencies, and acts on cue. Every mission also has a point of no return—the point at which it is more of a risk to turn back and compromise the mission than it is to keep going.

The concept of a point of no return removes the option of not proceeding and replaces it with a plan. In other words, the plan for the point of no return eliminates the chance the SWAT team members will feel overwhelmed and not act or freeze. Winning by overwhelming their adversary has been a strategy used by armies for centuries—the army that shows up biggest, strongest, and fastest has the psychological and physical advantage.

Businesses as well as individuals can lose by being overwhelmed. Anyone can have a bad day—maybe the person woke up late and slowed a team's ability to accomplish the work on deadline that day. Or maybe someone makes a mistake on the job, then heads to their car to go home, only to have a flat tire or run out of gas. On top of that, perhaps their computer breaks down and the internet slows or goes down too.

It's not unheard of to have those kinds of problems and more in a day. Whatever the situation, overwhelm easily can overcome any of us without warning.

## The Science

From a scientific perspective, thought occurs in a loop. Overwhelm is a breakdown in that loop of thought, according to Col. John Boyd (1927–1997), a U.S. Air Force fighter pilot who flew F-86 fighter planes in the Korean War. Boyd also deconstructed and documented philosophies of how we think in combat and, ultimately, our decision-making process in life. He calls the process the OODA loop—Observe, Orient, Decide, Act.[4]

In combat, a fighter pilot observes or sees an enemy aircraft, then orients to its position and surroundings, decides how to attack, and then acts. By understanding this thought process, Boyd shortened the time it took for pilots to deal with dogfight situations and increased the efficiencies of U.S. pilots compared with the enemy. He also taught this philosophy and tactic at the U.S. Air Force Fighter Weapons School. His nickname was Forty-Second Boyd.

---

[4]Farnham Street Media, "The OODA Loop: How Fighter Pilots Make Fast and Accurate Decisions" (accessed May 25, 2021), https://fs.blog/2021/03/ooda-loop/.

Reportedly, with Boyd's approach to decision-making, pilots could engage an enemy within 40 seconds of contact. The OODA loop forced a decision that created quick action, thus eliminating overwhelm. Boyd also recognized that without this process, a pilot could experience overwhelm and give the enemy the upper hand. As an example, what does a fighter pilot do when two enemy planes are approaching? Most would feel overwhelmed, but not with the OODA process.

## Boyd's Lesson in Business

Boyd's process further reinforces the concept that if you can deconstruct any problem—including fear—you can think it through and prevent overwhelm with action. Similarly in business, one way to overtake the competition is to surprise and outthink them by creating blind spots—a gap in the OODA loop. That can provide an offensive advantage. A blind spot is a situation, gap, or occurrence that interrupts the thought process and must be dealt with first to move forward.

In the SWAT world, for example, a flash-bang distraction tossed into a room disrupts the OODA loop of the people inside. It creates a gap in the response capabilities and timing of the people in the room because likely they haven't planned for that noise/distraction. The flash bang overwhelms their sight, hearing, and equilibrium and creates a gap in their decision-making. Success can be as much about creating unplanned decisions as it is about sowing doubt in the mind of the competition.

Blind spots occur in life—sometimes intentionally, sometimes not. A blind spot might consist of missing an option, overlooking a process, or simply not seeing an opportunity or challenge. That momentary gap in the OODA loop created by the blind spot can create an advantage.

However, we should learn to not overthink our reactions to blind spots. Rather than feel overwhelmed and freeze with inaction, we must quickly process the interruption and take action. Even in the face of blind spots, it's necessary to act, to move forward to prevent overwhelm. Action, after all, creates perspective that breaks down overwhelm in the decision-making process. Observe, orient, decide, act. Start thinking instead of shutting down and once again start with a win.

Businesses disrupt the OODA loop of competitors with product announcements and unanticipated releases, lawsuit filings, or new marketing pieces. When we see a business react to a competitor's actions, that business's OODA loop has been disrupted. Watch for it and don't allow your OODA loop to be impacted. Stay the course with your strategy with adjustments as needed, not reactions.

RE/MAX disrupted the OODA loop of its competitors at a major industry convention in November 1994 when its co-founder, Dave Liniger, and another great leader in the company, Mike Ryan, announced the RE/MAX Satellite Network. The network would provide training and programming to franchised brokerages via satellite broadcast. At that time this was unheard of in the industry and the only way to get real-time training to real estate agents in the field. The competition had to react, and did. RE/MAX's announcement became the buzz at the convention, and most of the other major real estate companies at the show ended up announcing that they, too, were going to have a real satellite network. Ryan said he knew then that we had a unique competitive advantage.[5]

Since that time, the real estate industry, like other industries, has faced a back-and-forth of innovative OODA disruptions. That's part of doing business. Expect it, prepare for it, and learn to operate on both sides of the spectrum. If you anticipate OODA loop disruptions, you operate from a confidence of capability to act, not from a position of being forced to react.

---

[5]Carol Patton, "RE/MAX: Training With a Competitive Advantage," via satellite, June 1, 2005 (accessed May 1, 2021), https://www.satellitetoday.com/telecom/2005/06/01/remax-training-with-a-competitive-advantage/.

# MULTIDIMENSIONAL APPROACH

Understanding the importance of a holistic approach to success helps create an awareness of potential blind spots, too. Then we can act to either avoid them or leverage them to create more opportunity.

In a business negotiation, for example, a blind spot can ultimately be an awakening to greater possibilities. The objection that surfaces in a discussion or negotiation can signal a gap in communications or in the capability of a process or product. The blind spot could lead to a new product or new way of accelerating the sales process.

## Ultimate Blind Spot

"We've always done it that way" is the biggest blind spot in business. Instead of being chained to the past, we need to reexplore how we do business. Today especially, people have an appetite for change in business and in life. That means they are more open to trying new business opportunities and efficiencies.

Just a year or so ago, the idea of everyone working from home seemed ridiculous. Now, the chorus everyone is singing is, "Do we have to go back into the office?" The answer, as we all have learned, is somewhere in the middle and a mix of both.

Humble leaders ask their teams to point out the blind spots, accept the feedback, and go with the solutions. You must execute and take action to keep the Beast at bay.

## Minimize It

However, rather than react immediately with tried-and-true processes, consider a multidimensional approach to minimize the blind spots. Consider the following:

- How might your competitors approach the same challenge? Why?
- Think about how your company formerly handled the same problem.

- If we reinvent our approach, how might we better handle the challenge?

A word of caution: Simply because a process is old and ingrained doesn't mean it's not a sound approach to deal with the challenge. Many businesses spend valuable time trying to reinvent perfectly sound processes rather than scaling those processes and increasing their efforts and resources. The trend today is to find a "fresh" way to do something. It somehow feels good to know your way is better than the previous way. But ultimately, don't ever forsake the knowledge that contributed to the current way.

# THE 80 PERCENT RULE

Perfection is yet another enemy of action. Too often people fail to act because they're not satisfied that a plan is foolproof or that the action will solve the problem completely. Remember, everything we do in life has some risk, including doing nothing. Done—as in a job or task—at 80 percent—is better than never finishing because you're too concerned about ensuring that the job or task is 100 percent perfect. That goes for the majority of tasks in life and business. Shoot for perfect and get done. It's a balance.

As I was growing up, my father always taught me to measure twice and cut once. That's a woodworking adage that reduces the probability of miscutting a piece of wood. Doublecheck your measurements before cutting, and then cut the wood quickly before you forget the measurements.

That's a wise approach to life, too. Make a plan, check it twice, and execute—take action. In other words, take the steps ahead of time to eliminate overwhelm and delay, and then just do it.

# DON'T IGNORE CHALLENGES

Don't ever think that if you ignore a problem, it will go away. However, sometimes dealing with one problem will fix or influence the solution of others, so choose wisely. For example, let's assume you're overweight. You have no energy to exercise, but you continue struggling to do so to lose weight. It's a vicious cycle.

But if you eat properly, you could gain the energy to exercise more easily and lose weight. The two problems fix each other—nutrition leads to energy, which leads to exercise, which leads to health. Similarly, just as victories add up to create great positive momentum for a sports team or individual, unaddressed problems create their own negative momentum. The more challenges left unattended, the more overwhelmed a person can become, and their performance and decision-making skills decline.

Problems compound just as solutions do. Try combining your problems and solutions together. Think about how you could address one problem and fix another at the same time. For example, your kids are having problems at home. Instead of addressing each issue separately, consider one family meeting to create greater alignment and clarity on expectations among the kids. That saves you from having to chase each problem individually.

Life is full of challenges that come up at the most inopportune times. Often we see multiple real or perceived threats, and we freeze. We get overwhelmed. Our emotions spiral out of control, and literally nothing gets done to address the challenge.

But there is a fix for this leadership showstopper. We can prevent our foundation of training and understanding from crumbling in the face of pressure, and we can begin to grow and learn instead. It all begins with understanding how your emotions work, how to align solutions, and how to take action. Remember, when faced with overwhelm, deconstruct the problems one step at a time and then act.

## EMOTIONAL CONTROL

A SWAT officer about to breach a building is scared. So is the staffer about to make the presentation of their lifetime to a company's board of directors, and the speaker waiting to go on stage before thousands of people. Yet each of those individuals follows through.

## Trained Responses

Each takes action because they trust themselves and their processes. Each has trained and knows they can get the job done. They work hard to understand, observe, and make the right decisions. The reality is that action overcomes emotions—especially fear. Leaders train themselves to make commitments and follow through on them.

You can, too. You can train yourself to start with a win by starting with a plan or process, a small commitment, and then moving on to more and more and more. Before you know it, you're well on the road to success and beyond that point of no return I mentioned earlier. You also can train yourself to take such actions as and when necessary.

## Psychology of Decision-Making

Earl Miller is an expert on decision-making skills and short-term memory. He's a professor of neuroscience at the Picower Institute for Learning and Memory in the Department of Brain and Cognitive Sciences at Massachusetts Institute of Technology. Miller found that the prefrontal cortex portion of our brains controls how we respond to situations. Our framework for making those decisions comes from repetition and results. Certain cues help activate certain actions in our brains.[6]

In other words, we build habits to activate an action step in our brains. Our decisions become subconscious. We rely on our training, processes, and known frameworks for solutions, focusing our energy on overcoming the challenge as opposed to rationalizing a way out of it.

---

[6]Earl K. Miller, "Working Memory 2.0: And the Network Dynamics of Cognitive Control," University of Cambridge MRC Chaucer Club, December 3, 2020, https://ekmillerlab.mit.edu/videos/.

## FORGET THE EASY WAY

Too often people make excuses to not do something difficult or challenging. They claim their inabilities or society is what prevents them from taking action. Leaders learn to override tendencies to go for the easy and instead embrace the challenging. They seek opportunity instead of ease and understand that pursuing opportunity creates new levels of fulfillment in life. This is how you party with the Beast to start with a win.

Think of the last time you tried something a little uncomfortable. Maybe it was cooking a new dish that turned into an amazing dinner or going to your boss and asking to be the project lead and then killing it. There are inherent satisfactions in life that give you confidence and deepen your relationship with your inner fears. These deeper relationships open new doors of confidence that lead to more actions on your part and build momentum to your next great win.

Don't miss an opportunity. If the Beast has crushed your dreams and aspirations, you need to change the framework for decisions in your mind and accomplish what you want to accomplish. Don't let anyone tell you, "You can't." Remember, life is about "I can." That simple phrase changes how your body deploys confidence and how you make your next move.

## CHANGING YOUR MINDSET

Deploying a change in mindset is a physical activity. It's a conscious micro action or micro commitment that makes a big difference.

Occasionally we all have a rough morning. Maybe you're facing a series of heavy challenges at work, or perhaps you spilled coffee on your clothes or had an argument with a spouse or fellow worker, or all of the above. Whatever the trigger, the domino effect of Beastly misfortunes happens in life, and we must make the conscious effort to change the effect.

# HIT RESET

One morning recently I left for the gym and definitely wasn't happy. Nothing was going my way. The farther I drove down the road and the more I thought about my problems, the madder I got. I worked myself up to the point where I was physically angry. The Beast was in full attack mode, which meant I wouldn't get much done that day.

That was the signal it was time to talk with my Beast. I turned on some soothing classical music and kept repeating aloud, "I am happy." "I am happy." "I am happy." I was in the car alone, talking to myself, intentionally smiling, and even laughing. Sounds ridiculous, but it worked. By the time I arrived at the gym my "conversation" had truly changed my day. It was uplifting, and I was a renewed person.

It is that simple to change our thoughts. Challenges do not go away; they just become clearer and more manageable when you remove emotional overwhelm. You tame the Beast within through conscious actions. For me that day, the challenges were still present, but my conscious reset enabled me to separate my feelings from my ability to handle the problems at hand. With renewed clarity and a decision-making system for actions, I could deal with anything. I was starting with a win.

# YOUR TURN

Try the reset sometime. Give yourself a break. No matter who we are or what our vocation, we can only perform one conscious act at a time. Separating the negativity from the challenges helps us to do that.

When you feel like the Beast is gaining on you, stop, and consciously dial down your negative emotions by replacing them with the positive. It takes a strong person to hit the reset button before a problem causes damage. The challenge is to figure out what reset works best for you so that you can turn fear into love. And beyond the attitude reset button, you better reset your humility, too, because it may take an apology or an extension of peace to complete the process.

## CONSCIOUS RESPONSE

Getting angry or overwhelmed are conscious acts themselves. Overwhelm is the frustration we experience when we try to perform too many conscious acts at once or when we face a seemingly unsolvable challenge. When we stop and reset our minds, then move forward one step at a time, we simplify the challenge and ultimately accomplish the task.

When emotions threaten to overwhelm you, unplug. Make a change to be what you want to be—happy and clear-minded. Don't feel weird about stopping to reset; we all need to occasionally step back to better understand how to pursue the positive. Life is about getting your mind right before anything else positive can happen.

## HELP ALONG THE WAY

All kinds of tools are out there to help with an attitude reset. Instead of listening to classical music and talking to yourself, try sitting down and journaling about positive aspects of your life, what brings you joy, or what you're grateful for.

Meditation is another positive action, either via traditional methods or an app on your mobile device. For the latter, I like Calm, focus@ will, or Headspace. It doesn't require lots of time, either. Perhaps 10 minutes of meditation can provide you a full day of fulfillment and positivity.

Some people may choose to take a walk, outdoors or indoors, or try some other form of exercise to reset. Still others might take a few minutes to devote to something entirely different to switch those gears in their mind.

Since work from home during the pandemic became the norm, many of us have had to hyper-focus on challenges associated with the new workplace. Those challenges could be overwhelming due to business problems or the depression that might result from lack of human contact in an office setting. Whatever the reason, I had to find my "happy place" many times in 2020.

This will continue because the emotional transformation is powerful. Sometimes that transformation comes from sitting in the woods behind my house listening to classical music for a few minutes, taking a short stroll with my dogs for some fresh air, or even sitting on the floor with my eyes closed for a quick meditation session.

These ideas on how to find that "happy place" aren't unique to me, either. Conversations with other business leaders around the world on video meetups frequently include ideas on how to reset and recharge.

How have you learned to find your reset button? Keep it handy; it makes you a better leader.

## THINK POSITIVE

The more we think we can, the more we can. This is a trained behavior. Have you ever noticed that some people are perpetually positive? They always win, make progress, have great relationships, are healthy, and enjoy their jobs and friends.

These are the super-achievers. They understand how to control their feelings and realize how the brain works when it comes to fear and love; they want to have an amazing relationship with their Beast, and as a result, they have an amazing life. They are the people who get in line in the morning to party with the Beast. They don't tolerate the rest of the distractions in life. They acknowledge that negativity and naysayers exist, but that doesn't affect their happiness and productivity. They choose their own results.

## INTERPERSONAL RELATIONSHIPS

Interpersonal relationships have fallen victim to the virtual workplace and e-business. That's unfortunate because, as I mentioned, relationships are essential in today's competitive business environment.

In times of crisis, especially, isolation can lead to emotions running high. When that happens, often people stop making decisions, to the detriment of the business.

## UNDERSTANDING

Understanding these emotions—fear among them—and employing personal attention and appreciation help address those challenges and rekindle the personal relationships. To bring teams back together and bolster interpersonal relationships, companies may turn to regular virtual happy hours and get-togethers as well as other virtual group experiences to reconnect and reenergize workplaces.

Traditionally some leaders have opted for bowling, softball teams, golf, company picnics, or even getting together regularly outside of work to toss a frisbee. However a company or its leaders choose to foster team spirit and camaraderie, it doesn't have to be elaborate, but it does have to be intentional.

Since RE/MAX is an international company, our conventions always feature a parade of flags. Agents from all the countries represented march around the convention center waving their countries' flags. It's a great example of sharing national pride with your peers.

## COMMUNICATION

Communication, though, is the foundation for relationships, period. In addition to the convention parade and because real estate is a business of referrals, our agents gather to celebrate, network, and develop relationships that break down real and imagined barriers and generate business across borders.

When there's a business relationship challenge, the solution starts with cranking up communications. Whether that means daily, weekly, bimonthly, or monthly meetings doesn't matter. The important part is to develop a happy cadence that fulfills a customer's needs and desire to maintain the relationship.

I had a customer who told me he thought we didn't care about his team. So I made sure that we started regular weekly communications with them, and almost immediately his team was 10 times happier, all because of communication. Not long after that, though, he asked me to stop calling so much because they were so motivated that they didn't have as much time to chat.

# THE STRUGGLERS

So often in the workplace, virtual or otherwise, we see others struggling. Chances are they're doing battle with their own Beast. In fact, helping these strugglers is one of the biggest challenges facing a leader.

Problems at work almost never start at work. Remember, how we do one thing is how we do all things. People who struggle on the job often are upset in their personal lives first. They complain; they are miserable; they have troubles in relationships, and with their health.

Absolutely as a leader, it's your responsibility to reach out to these people to help. A great approach is to sit down with the person and let them know that you feel something outside of your control is challenging their ability to perform to their full potential. And you want to help because you think they have so much more potential than they realize. Then I ask, "Is everything OK in the other aspects of your life?" Again, the idea is "people don't care what you know until they know you care."

A leader should offer the individual the help available through the business—employee assistance and wellness programs, for example. Realistically, though, not everyone is willing to participate in their own rescue. It's back to the "I can" as opposed to the excuses. People who aren't willing to try to be happy and productive aren't.

Often these same people turn to self-help seminars and counseling because they don't know how to participate in their own rescue. Unfortunately, though, many leave those experiences with the frustration that they *could* be better but are not right now. The reason: They are unwilling to embrace "I can" and prefer to embrace excuses.

If this is the case, the employee should be informed that they aren't performing at the level your high-performance team and you, the leader, expect. Emphasize you are there to help, but the rest of the team and those impacted by the team have performance expectations, and if those expectations aren't met, dismissal is an option.

## THE FLIP SIDE

The reality is that there are people in life who don't want to do the work or who want to fire off an attack actively or passively to avoid doing the work, whatever the work is. These people blame their situation on others and find a way to leverage their active or passive bullying to get their way. It's a learned habit. As a leader it's your responsibility not to tolerate such behavior.

But keep in mind, people who are hurting try to hurt others. For clarity, let's flip the words. People who try to hurt others are hurting. That's so true, especially when it comes to hiring or retention of employees.

Pain, whether emotional or physical, is a virus some people try to pass around. Its vaccine is love and happiness. I'm not trying to be fluffy or touchy/feely; rather, I'm a realist. Empower over enable—leaders must empower people to help themselves, not enable them to do the least possible.

---

### Leadership Takeaways

- Our emotions dominate us through fear and self-doubt and threaten to overshadow all we do.
- Harnessing self-doubt is among the greatest strengths we have. Allowing fear to rule our lives is the greatest weakness.
- Fear can be deconstructed and defeated. Fear is only as deep as the mind allows.
- Appreciation is magic.

- When you act with integrity and work in your people's best interests, you can fail and learn. You can make it through difficulties. People respect your ability not to succeed in everything, and they don't fault you personally for less-than-successful outcomes.

- If you can deconstruct any problem—including fear—you can think it through and prevent overwhelm with action.

- Meet fear with love.

- Perfection is the enemy of action.

- Don't ever think that if you ignore a problem, it will go away. Just as victories add up to create great positive momentum for a sports team or individual, so do unaddressed problems create their own negative momentum. The more challenges left unattended, the more overwhelmed a person can become, and their performance and decision-making skills decline.

- You can train yourself to start with a win by starting with a plan or process, a small commitment, and then moving on to more and more and more.

- The more we think we can, the more we can. That's a trained behavior.

- Getting angry or overwhelmed are conscious acts. Overwhelm is the frustration we experience when we try to perform too many conscious acts at once or when we face a seemingly unsolvable challenge. In the face of overwhelm, take time to stop and reset your mind. Then you can simplify the challenge and ultimately accomplish the task.

- Problems at work almost never start at work. People who struggle on the job often are upset in their personal lives first. They complain; they are miserable; they have troubles in relationships, and with their health.

## CHAPTER 4

# Be a Sponge

*"If you're not moving forward, you're losing ground."*

—Adam Contos

**F**or years I always walked into classrooms and presentations and sat in the back of the room. Then one day I walked into a classroom and sat in the front.

When you walk into a presentation or class or another form of potential learning, do you head to the front of the room or the back? That's not a trick question.

Have you ever noticed the difference in those people around you when you sit in the back versus the front? Chances are those in the front of the room don't struggle as much to understand a concept, while those in the back often do. The bottom line is that when we take learning very seriously, we learn. When we don't, we struggle.

When I was growing up, I used to purposely sit in different parts of a classroom and explore the differences in people around me. It was a great idea and sounds good, but my execution was a bit flawed. If I wasn't interested in a class, my grades showed it. When I became interested in learning—a lifelong learner—I became very successful. I wanted to be the best that I could be in all aspects of my job—consulting, contracts, sales, marketing, executive leadership, and more.

No matter the situation or the circumstance, when we intentionally seek out learning and challenge ourselves, we become better at who we are and what we do, and we come away with a win. But soaking up knowledge is only half the equation.

Distilling it into something valuable for others to use in their lives and then sharing it creates the real value. By sharing your learnings, you help others create their own successes and start with their own wins. That's what leaders do.

## NARC MARKETING 101

While with the Douglas County (Colorado) Sheriff's Office, I spent two years as an undercover cop with the South Metro Drug Task Force. With training from the federal Drug Enforcement Administration, I worked the streets of the Denver metropolitan area undercover buying drugs. It was the best sales training imaginable. That's right, sales training.

This was NARC Marketing 101. Of course, I don't advocate this approach for anyone, but these were my missions, and I took advantage of what I could learn from each one. I became an expert at how to proactively meet strangers, convince them I was a trustworthy associate and friend, and get them to risk everything by selling me illegal drugs that, if they were caught doing so, could put them in prison for years.

It was highly stressful as well as sad to see so many people on the downhill slide toward loss of their kids, financial ruin, and, too often, overdose or suicide. As cops, we did what we could to help these people, but ultimately it was on them to lift themselves up and save their own lives and lifestyles. Each of us has to participate in our own rescues—whether from drugs or fear or inaction. Whatever the situation, the onus is on each of us to help ourselves.

# THE VALUE OF SHARING KNOWLEDGE

Working as a street cop and then undercover taught me tremendous empathy, something I tried hard then, and continue to try, to share with others daily.

## Cop Stories

Learning empathy as a cop was an enlightening education. In police academy, we learned to talk to people in a robotic, calculated manner to avoid any accusations of emotional interaction or favoritism. I equate the training to imitating Detective Joe Friday in the old police television drama *Dragnet*. Joe always said to the victims, "Just the facts, ma'am" as the victim was trying to tell their story.

Stories, with their emotional descriptions and feelings, often mean more to the person telling them than do the facts that the police attempt to gather. Yet the police must quickly get the information and move on. Allowing people to express their feelings before the facts was the solution.

Working in narcotics also posed unique opportunities to learn about facts, feelings, and sales. Undercover I had to initially earn someone's trust to do a deal with them, and they were always nervous about the relationship. The trust-earning game happened primarily through empathy that had to be maintained throughout the contact with the person—from the drug purchase to the arrest and beyond to gain their cooperation after the arrest. There were quite a few interesting (and lasting) lessons learned in understanding, role-playing, empathy, and deal-making.

As narcotics agents, we usually went into areas where residents had complained of drug activity. We had to fit in and find out what was happening. Sounds like sales, right? Through the relationships we built locally, we ended up discovering drug distribution networks—or opportunities. It's similar to the business of entering a new sales market—go in, meet the players, learn about them, and begin the business processes due to the shared empathy and desire to accomplish mutual tasks.

As a narc, the goal was the exchange of drugs for money. In business, the goal is the exchange of something of value for something else of value. Both goals involve an empathy game. And it's the Feel Felt Found sales process that I discovered as a cop by studying sales techniques. Once I sat down with someone arrested for drug sales, it wasn't a conversation along the lines of "You violated this section of the law, you have the right to remain silent," and so on. While the legal processes were followed, emotional bridges were built as well. My process also included, "I know how you feel being caught. I'm sure it's difficult and I care. I too have felt bad, but what I have found is that there is always a solution. Let's explore that together."

People want to be heard, felt, and understood. As a police officer, whether the case was a narcotics drug buy or a SWAT operation, "Just the facts ma'am" might have been good for a TV show in the 1950s, but it's not the way to care about people you are trying to help.

When you feel for others—empathy—they want to contribute to the solution. That's whether you're a cop on a collar or a sales agent on a business call.

## FREE AND WITHOUT EXPECTATIONS

The real value of learning and having great knowledge lies in giving it back—so much so that people notice. The goal isn't praise or personal recognition; it's free giving of knowledge without expectations to help others.

That's how Dave Liniger built his RE/MAX global empire—by helping people get better. Dave always says he likes to help people find their greatest potential above and beyond what they ever thought they could achieve.

In my learnings and career, for example, Dave never stops teaching me. When I first met him in my early years as a deputy sheriff, he would join me on the street for ride-alongs in my squad car. He liked the excitement of a front-row seat to what was happening, plus we had great conversations. He shared with me what books and articles to read, and so much more.

I would join him to watch televised NASCAR races at his home. These sessions turned into leadership lessons as Dave, a former team owner, used the race teams to explain leadership concepts.

We were watching the Daytona 500 in 2001 when Dale Earnhardt tragically died on the last lap. Dave instantly knew what had happened based on the dynamics of the crash and response of those on the track. He was a master at reading people, their emotions, body language, intentions, and kindness or lack thereof.

## MODELING THE BEHAVIOR

Today at age 76, Dave is still a great role model. He's incredibly curious and conscious, always sharing articles and books, and he enjoys discussing leadership and business principles. He's hungry for knowledge, and it shows. I regularly sit with Dave at his kitchen table discussing our latest leadership or business case study or book. He is and always will be a lifelong sponge, and in fact he is the inspiration behind the title of this chapter.

---

*"Don't be a know-it-all; be a give-it-all."*

—Adam Contos

---

He's also perfected the gentle yet intentional art of learning and sharing knowledge. That's how true leaders lead. They give, but never expect. They learn and do first, too, because people follow the actions of their leaders.

Dave exemplifies the leader who knows that part of his job is to enroll those around him in self-improvement by providing new knowledge, problem-solving capabilities, and perspective. Combining these thoughts and emotions creates the drive, excitement, determination, and actions necessary for each of us to grow.

## THE RIGHT WAY TO SHARE KNOWLEDGE

- *Notice*
- *Understand*
- *Explore*
- *Learn*
- *Act*
- *Give*

# THE GROWTH MINDSET OR NOT

One day, while still in law enforcement, I walked into a meeting of fellow officers, one of whom had just returned from a training seminar. The idea of a peer with new knowledge and insights to share sounds great. But there's another side to the story.

I remember looking around the room at everyone, including the officer with his newly learned insights, and quickly realizing that my peers were afraid to say much. They knew that those among us opposed to change would either go on the offensive or listen to the idea, gently agree, then do nothing with it. No matter which scenario ensued, however, any hope of growth from new knowledge collapsed before it began.

# PAIN OF CHANGE

Some people simply don't like change; they don't want to learn anything new, and they definitely aren't interested in getting better at what they do. Rather, they opt for the comfort of doing things the same way as they always have been done.

These recalcitrants among us can be any age. They resent and even lash out at others who strive to learn and grow, and they equate change with pain. One of their common refrains: "Yeah, right; here comes the new way of doing it."

Remember, the reference earlier to "A rut is nothing more than a shallow grave"? Believe it. I refer to these people who don't like change or anyone who pushes for change as ROD—Retired on Duty.

# MINDSET

Picture this: Your computer with all your important work information breaks down. It's a frustrating situation made worse because you're in the middle of dealing with an emotional and difficult customer. You try to contact the tech service people to fix the problem. But of course, the technician takes his time getting back to you.

When the technician, ROD, finally shows up, he's of little help. "Not much we can do about this," ROD says. "It happens a lot. We probably won't be able to do anything about it."

Perhaps if ROD and his team had the ability to dig deeper into the malfunction with the help of the latest technology and available techniques, they could solve the problem. But they don't know how to do that because they didn't take the time to learn how. ROD's team just wants to punch the time clock, do the minimum necessary to get by, and then go home when the shift ends. Their goal is to burn days off the calendar until the magic hour of retirement. If you ask ROD when he's going to retire, he'll probably be able to tell you the exact number of years, days, and hours.

ROD is a tough mindset for me, and probably you, to grasp. But that doesn't mean we don't see it all the time. The reality is that every industry, business, and sector of society—public or private—runs the risk of promoting RODs and RODAs (the female version) if the particular organization allows it. Too many do.

What stops the RODs and RODAs from taking over? The answer is simple—a growth mindset of excellence starting from the top. Leaders have the choice to raise the bar and create an environment that encourages personal growth.

# START WITH A WIN

Now imagine a different scenario with your broken computer. A different technician shows up and does everything he can to solve the problem. He's patient and utilizes the latest in technology and communications to search for trends and similarities to resolve the situation instead of just recording the facts, saying nope, and moving on. He taps into his network to determine if the same thing has happened before. He researches online for similar problems. He owns the outcome of this call. It's not my computer; it's his computer, and he wants to know what's wrong with it. We all should handle challenges that way.

Unfortunately, that's not what always happens. Supervisors who send their employees to training classes often say to me, "What if we make them better and they leave?" My response is always the same, "What if we don't and they stay?"

We don't want organizations made up of RODs and RODAs. Seniority shouldn't mean more than performance. People who perform well should be compensated at a markedly higher rate than those who simply exist. And those who just exist should be on an exit plan if they won't try to become better at what they do.

Organizations should not tolerate mediocrity. Instead, the goal should be to encourage calculated risk-taking to create smart growth.

## WISE VERSUS SILLY

Early in my law enforcement training someone shared a rather long but telling story:

> Five monkeys were placed in a room where a banana hung from the ceiling. Underneath the banana was a ladder. When the monkeys tried to climb the ladder, they were sprayed with ice cold water. They immediately climbed back down the ladder without the banana.

Several more attempts to reach the banana netted the same results—cold water and no banana.

One by one, each monkey was replaced with a new monkey. From this point on, though, the monkeys weren't sprayed with cold water if they tried to climb the ladder. Whenever a new monkey was brought in to replace an original monkey, the newcomer would try to climb up to reach the banana. But its peers would pull it down because they remembered the water spray. The new monkey assumed the others didn't want it to get the banana.

Eventually even the new monkeys who had never been sprayed with cold water joined in pulling their fellow monkeys off the ladder. When all the original monkeys were replaced, the newer ones still could not climb up to get the banana without being pulled down by the others.

This epitomizes the mindset "We have always done it this way," so no need to change.

Think about the following questions:

- Does your organization operate like the group of monkeys?
- Do supervisors throw "cold water" on employees who come up with new ideas?
- More importantly, how does someone get the banana if everyone thinks it's not allowed?

I once worked with a leader who limited innovation and change in the company and among employees. That attitude is made worse because it not only prevents change but also discounts the feelings of those involved. When someone in the company had a new idea on how to do something or was struggling with the outcomes of past limitations—and like the monkey, couldn't reach the banana—this leader's response invariably was, "It is what it is; get used to it."

What a frustrating and dead-end way to live.

## CONFUSING CHANGE WITH SUCCESS

Of course, changing simply to change isn't the right approach, either. But not seeking improvement, personal or otherwise, because someone is opposed to change isn't the right way.

Change doesn't automatically ensure success. In fact, sometimes, change makes things worse if, for example, you or your company have already found a great formula for doing something. That's why it's so important to calculate and test changes on a small scale before implementing a company-wide shift.

In other words, if you're considering a process change, continue to operate your business as is while testing the changes on a small-scale with a parallel version of the business. It's much like what happens during major court trials. Jury and court consultants create mock juries similar to the real jury and run a parallel trial to study different approaches and techniques.

At one point we considered changing a pricing model in a business we operate. So we tried out 14 different pricing models on a number of participants. We found that the solution wasn't a new pricing model; it was the approach to operations and value delivery.

Change isn't always good. But creating a culture that prevents change and knowledge improvement is always bad. Next time, try taking the approach, "We seek knowledge to create necessary change," instead of saying, "We don't do change for the sake of change."

When you fail to grow, it's too late to change.

## TRY TEACHING IT

One of the greatest ways to keep learning and improving at whatever you do—whether sales, negotiating, people skills, leadership, training, listening, designing, and so much more—is to teach it. Teaching improves your own understanding of the idea and how to better articulate it to others. Shoot a cell phone video of you teaching, too. Do you understand what you're saying on the video?

Could you learn from you? If not, don't quit; try again until you get it right.

# TROUBLESHOOT, DIAGNOSE, EDUCATE

Teaching is not only telling and training; it's troubleshooting and diagnosing what defines success in a particular situation or action. Leaders do that day in and day out.

Everyone in a classroom learns differently, so a teacher also must be able to recognize how to bypass an individual's roadblocks to learning before engaging that person's interest enough to convey an idea and help them understand it. Leaders do this every day in every situation.

# SAME STEPS TO SUCCESS

The subject being taught doesn't really matter. Learning can be intimidating whether the subject is SWAT operations and security or how to write a business plan, fulfill customer needs, or negotiate a contract. I've taught them all.

Whatever is being taught, the principles of deconstructing success are the same; the frameworks for success are the same, as are the human response and emotional principles. It's simply the industry and what is at risk that are variables. As a reminder, to deconstruct the steps:

- Assess the situation.
- Identify the challenges.
- Plan the response.
- Take the appropriate action.

# IDENTIFYING OPPORTUNITIES

So, if you're interested in improving at what you do, building your leadership skills, and winning at the same time, consider teaching.

Plenty of opportunities are out there—some volunteer, others with financial incentives. The win, though, is not the money; it's the knowledge you gain from sharing and learning simultaneously. Be a sponge.

Community colleges are almost always looking for instructors, as are industry groups and community centers. Online and volunteer opportunities abound, too. Google "teaching opportunities" in your field, and see where it leads you.

## FREE SHARING

When I began my part-time security consulting business, I shared knowledge free of charge to deliver value. I liked the feeling of knowing I helped people stay safe. Free sharing is also a great relationship builder. In fact, providing value to someone else is one of the most overlooked approaches to developing close relationships with customers. Providing value creates reciprocity.

Robert Cialdini, PhD, a social psychology professor at Arizona State University, examines reciprocity as one of the six principles of influence in his book *Influence: The Psychology of Persuasion*. Those principles are:

- Reciprocity
- Commitment/consistency
- Social proof
- Authority
- Liking
- Scarcity

Humans, says Cialdini, are wired to return favors and repay debts.[1] When we give freely, we receive in return. That's why when

[1] Robert Cialdini, *Influence: The Psychology of Persuasion* (New York: Harper Business, rev. ed., 2006).

someone visits a blog or reads an article posted by a business, that person often is inclined to purchase from that business—to subconsciously return the favor.

When I began my security consulting business, I hoped that giving great information would create a return on this investment of time and knowledge and would stimulate business. I wrote articles for publications, sent sample security brochures to companies, and met with business leaders to help them keep their businesses, employees, and customers safe—all at no charge. I received consistently positive feedback on the value I delivered. That value translated into conversations about transactions and consulting help.

The value I provided was knowledge that I had researched, recorded, documented, and repurposed to relate to the customers' industries or challenges. Consultants generally find answers for companies, and that's what I did. I was a solution seller. But, to sell solutions, you must first give away knowledge to open the door for transaction discussions. That's where most businesses fail. They don't want to give away their best advice; they want to sell it. However, no one wants to buy your advice until the other free advice works for them.

# CHALLENGES ARE OPPORTUNITIES

As I've discussed, no matter the obstacles, when we damn the Beast, step up to the plate, and take on the challenge, we can hit a home run. That's a promise.

### You Can Do It!

When I joined RE/MAX, first as a consultant and then as a full-time employee, I didn't have a college degree. The outlook for me rising to the top of leadership at a multinational public company wasn't very good, no matter what I did or who I knew. Then the leadership at RE/MAX suggested I get an MBA, and that presented a new set of challenges.

But challenges are surmountable. Think SPA—Stress, Planning, Action. I learned that some colleges and universities offer experienced business executives without undergraduate degrees the option to apply for a waiver and then to earn a master's degree.

Going back to school is a life/career changer. If you have the business experience but not the degree, don't let the Beast keep you from furthering your education. Whatever it is you want to accomplish academically, with the right attitude and perseverance you can score the win.

## Expect Tough Times

Admittedly, working full time and going to school nights and weekends was taxing. But I promised myself that I would make the most of this new opportunity. I read everything they gave me, attended every class I could, and did all the homework. Any class I could not attend—I missed very few—I met with the professor and arranged to do the work ahead of time.

How could I do all that? Simple: I utilized the same systems and processes that I needed to run a business and plugged them into accomplishing the schoolwork. I was determined to win! It was effective, and I graduated with a 4.0. Anything is possible, any problem surmountable with the right attitude and the right approach.

For those who are in excuse mode and figure going to school and working full time is just too much, ditch the "I can't" and think again. I also had a wife and three small children at the time. My relationship with my family was supportive and happy, and my career thrived.

# A MATTER OF SYSTEMS

Faced with extreme challenges, double down on your systems. Those systems are the playbook for life amassed from all your missions. Overcoming the problems and taking action for a win is not about the difficulty of the challenge; it's a question of how focused your systems are to solve the problems.

Systems overcome challenges, so we all need solid systems in place for our lives and businesses to become more successful. Most importantly in this day of constant distractions, systems keep us focused. We have enough time in the day to complete what we need to, but somehow we always seem to throw in time-wasting distractions and then say, "I ran out of time."

Maybe you did run out of time. But it's because you didn't use your systems to get the necessities done first. Focus!

When you become a police officer, a real estate agent, a Marine, or almost any other profession, you learn to use a framework or systems for success in any of your encounters. As a cop, it could be the procedure to write a report, make a traffic stop, direct traffic, or investigate a crime. In real estate, agents follow several steps when they do listing presentations. As a Marine, you're up with reveille and have certain requirements when it comes to your living quarters or how you line up for review, maintain equipment or knowledge, or even enter a battle.

Essentially, in all these situations, you set expectations and communicate the systems or processes to yourself and those working with you to address the situation or challenge in the allocated time. Then you follow through for the win.

## LOGIC, NOT EMOTION

Frameworks or systems help us all maintain level heads to act logically and with kindness. Leaders can't allow situations or people to upset them to the point of reacting emotionally. Emotions, after all, are like dominos. One falls and triggers a chain reaction of falling dominos. Keeping a cool head allows a person to focus on the situation and solve the challenge.

Chances are we all know someone who "wings it" regularly in business and life. That's unfortunate because their lack of consistency—that is, lack of a framework—creates confusion and chaos. Do you know anyone who lives in chaos? Results are minimized, too, because when someone doesn't follow a process, it's impossible to know what works and what doesn't.

## SYSTEMS AND KNOWLEDGE

At the end of my MBA program, the professors asked for the one thought each student would like to share. My thought: You don't know what you don't know. While that may sound simplistic and obvious, it's really a reminder that each of us must aggressively seek knowledge. Plus, if we approach a challenge with hunger and humility, we will grow from it.

In school, every week was a new mission, just like a new SWAT call or a new business challenge. While all these missions taxed my discipline with time and choice management, I enjoyed the challenges. They were not easy, and they were not just procedural assignments. They required me to think, compare, and contrast while applying business pressures to situations just as happens in real business life. Afterward, I had to justify the outcomes and explain why I didn't pursue other options. The process sounds like a SWAT call—only in this case, it was an MBA call. The reality is that when challenges increase, so must our focus on accomplishment with the help of our systems and knowledge. If we don't have the information we need, we do the research necessary to find it. Then our leadership grows.

**Leadership Takeaways**

• No matter the situation or the circumstance, when we intentionally seek out learning and challenge ourselves, we become better at who we are and what we do, and we come away with a win.

• The real value of learning and having great knowledge lies in giving it back—so much so that people notice. The goal isn't praise or personal recognition; it's free giving of knowledge without expectations to help others.

- Organizations should not tolerate mediocrity. Instead, the goal should be to encourage calculated risk-taking to create smart growth.

- To improve your leadership skills, consider teaching a class. The subject doesn't matter; it's the process that's important because teaching is not only telling and training, but also troubleshooting and diagnosing what defines success in a particular situation or action. Leaders do that day in and day out.

- In order to sell solutions, you must first give away knowledge to open the door for transaction discussions. Too many businesses fail because they don't want to give away their best advice; they want to sell it. No one wants to buy your advice until the other free advice works for them.

- Faced with extreme challenges, double down on your systems. Those systems are the playbook for life amassed from all your missions.

- Emotions are like dominos—one falls and triggers a chain reaction of falling dominos. Keeping a cool head allows a person to focus on the situation and solve the challenge.

# CHAPTER 5

# Leadership Learnings

*"Want people to do something? Let them see you do it."*
—Adam Contos

**L**eadership is *freaking* hard! Whether you lead a team of one (yourself), 10, or 100,000, it's tough to command yourself to always strive to make the right series of choices that create actions others can observe and mirror. It's tough to maintain a dedicated direction and consistency in the face of opposition. And it's tough to fight the good fight then go home and lead yourself and your family. Then it's tough to get up every day and do it again. But it's also very rewarding if you allow it.

Real leadership, after all, is not about getting others to do what you want them to do. It's about modeling the behavior in yourself daily and then allowing others to find it within themselves to be at their best. If someone tries only to make others better without bettering themselves, those wins will remain elusive.

To help understand the job of a leader, imagine everyone yelling "no" at you at the same time. All this happens while you are trying to make critical decisions that affect your organization and all those individuals the organization touches. It's overwhelming and can stop action. Leading is choosing our actions and then accepting and learning from our results.

## AMAZING LEADERSHIP

Leadership makes an incalculable difference in an organization. An amazing leader provides a strong foundation and leads to a great organization. Leaders must be able to assess a situation and react appropriately and know when and how to take action even though those actions will not please everyone.

Today leaders don't have to face only the challenge itself; they face the emotional attack that goes along with it and must be able to balance the two in order to accomplish the task. Without proper understanding, observations, and decision-making skills, a leader lacks that strong foundation and makes poor decisions or hesitates to make decisions at all.

## TAKE THE TIME

Most true leaders don't rush into decisions. They watch, calculate, and gather solutions and options even though most people want them to run into the fray and make decisions immediately.

When a fire truck pulls up to the scene of a fire, the firefighters don't jump out and instantly charge into the blaze. They exit the truck, assess the situation, and calmly prepare to fight the fire. To the untrained, it might look like they're ho-hum about fighting the fire. But instead, they're developing an appropriate plan and situating their equipment to do their jobs effectively.

The same thing happens with a SWAT team on an operation. The team takes its time to do things not fast but smoothly. We had a saying: "Slow is smooth, smooth is quick, quick is fast." Leaders don't rush, they move in a calculated and patient manner.

That applies to more situations than just leadership. Rushed decisions are attempts to react, not act. Poor decisions come from rushed emotions. While something might "feel" like the right thing to do at the moment, it might not be the right decision. Yes, sometimes during an emergency we have to take action and at least make a statement like, "We understand the situation and are working on it."

## FEELINGS MATTER

Often the only thing people want to know is that you care. They want you to notice their emotional overwhelm, and the longer you wait to acknowledge it, the more they believe you don't care. (That attitude signals weak emotional judgment and impatience on their part.) Nonetheless, people want to transfer the burden of the problem to you because they assume that since you're not saying anything, you are part of the problem.

Don't allow yourself as a leader to be caught in a situation where you can't create strong solutions. At the same time, though, as a leader you can't ignore the feelings of those impacted by a situation.

The bottom line is that leaders who lead with emotion and reaction are not good leaders, even though people think they want those type of leaders. It's a double-edged sword a leader must learn to wield. Emotions matter, but we also must understand that when emotions run high, people tend to bulldoze their way through decisions or bully their way to get decisions from others. They get angry and frustrated, use emotional words, and curse. They lose their ability to see their way out of the situation and they make more bad decisions out of fear and anger. It's battling the Beast while trying to make decisions.

## PERSONAL QUEST

Leadership—like harnessing the Beast—is up to each of us as individuals. Many people have a misbelief in life that others are responsible for their successes or failures. Not so. It's the "I can" versus the excuses again. The bottom-line wins or learnings are up to each of us. Leadership is the same way. We don't really "learn" leadership; we become aware of and deploy the actions that create leading.

True leadership is earned through the constant hard work of demonstrating what you believe success looks like. Myriad studies and surveys analyze leadership; some offer good information, others not so. Often those designing and conducting the studies fail to account for the realities of business and the real-life world of emotions.

Many people talk about their leadership but fall short in practice. The more overwhelming a situation becomes, the more a leader:

- Must be physically, emotionally, and intellectually capable of leading to begin with
- Must be on point to lead through it holistically
- Must be clearer and more caring and confident in their actions
- Must be able to assess situations effectively to uncover blind spots as well as opportunities
- Should be transparent and vulnerable with a confidence that prevents vulnerability from being misinterpreted as weakness

## ACCOUNTABILITY

My missions in law enforcement as a leader and a follower reinforced the importance of accountability and of acting ethically, morally, legally, and in the best interests of humanity and community. There was no tolerance for inappropriate actions by anyone, and people were quick to act when they saw any.

Those are learnings that stuck. And that is where the transformation to true leadership happens—from experience to recognition to leadership.

---

*Leaders create action.*

*Action drives results.*

*Results overcome challenges.*

---

# EXPECTATIONS

People expect certain things from their leaders that are easier to state than execute. A leader's job is to impact as many people as possible to convey their message and magnify it to others. It's about building a movement. Leading is making decisions and taking actions, but it is also about creating positive motion, physically, emotionally, and professionally in the lives of others.

Leaders pull people away from fear (the Beast again) and into a comfortable reality. That reality could be chaos, but it is reality—get comfortable with it. The goal is for your people to know what's going on and not be afraid of it so that they can find contentment and confidence in themselves. Leaders find peace in what seems like chaos, and others discover this through the leadership. With that accomplished, they can get back to what they need to focus on—health, happiness, and productivity.

# CONFIDENCE

CEO mentor Darren Hardy shared with me that the greatest trait of a leader is confidence. Without confidence, people are guided by fear, the default emotion. And without confidence, people are unwilling to exert effort on anything. Instead, they're perpetually distracted by their doubts.

With confidence and a little action, we get direction and clarity that leads to progress out of the current challenge or to a realization that, challenge or not, we can function within the challenging environment and lessen the challenge in the process. Problem solved, or at least mitigated enough to resume action.

Of note, however, is to realize that there is a flip side to this approach. The big challenge is that leadership can be overwhelmed by what's required to maintain the confidence of others. Leaders, after all, are human. Leaders feel pressure build up like anyone else. Ideally, though, leaders have the ability to figuratively take a step back and focus.

# HOW TO DEVELOP CONFIDENCE

The good news is that we can develop confidence. I learned that way back in Marine boot camp.

In fact, as recruits we recited little confidence-building mantras every day. When we went into a classroom, for example, our platoon would recite something as we sat down, every single time we sat down: "Yea, though I walk through the shadow of the valley of death, I shall fear no one, for I am the biggest, baddest muther of them all."

We had another chant about not quitting that our platoon would recite on command: "On the plains of hostility lay the blackened bodies of countless millions who, on the dawn of victory, rested, and resting . . . died." This bit of mental programming is especially memorable and something to take along in life that applies whenever you lack confidence or ability or the will to continue the fight.

The mantra is a simple way to rewire your brain from doubt to confidence and push you into action or continued action with more intensity. Sometimes it provides the little extra patience to slow down and stay focused. Other times it offers the burst of necessary willpower. Whatever the purpose—even in the office when the day drags on and negotiations are nearing an impasse—that little extra dose of positivity works wonders.

# THE THREE CS OF LEADERSHIP

The best leaders focus on confidence, communication, and connection. Once there's confidence, it can be converted into action through communication. And confidence communicated is clarity.

## Hope

Once people have clarity, they have hope and can align to the movement of others and the goals of their leaders. In leadership-speak, hope is the culmination of action and the possibility of future results. It's where we find the opportunities—do this and likely you'll achieve that. Hope is fuel for action.

While hope is not the strategy, it is the energy. People generally will not act without hope unless they have extreme confidence in their leader. In fact, the No. 1 reason people purchase something is out of hope—hope for change, benefit, or solution. But beware of creating false hope. That generally happens when we set a finish line and anticipate exact results.

A great example of false hope comes from the pandemic. People began talking about everything "back to normal by" a certain date. That gave them hope that perpetuated until the date came and went, which dashed all hope and energy. People became frustrated with leadership and the information it was disseminating.

In reality, the solution—in this case, to the pandemic—required a process, not a destination. People want hope from leadership even when there clearly is not a fixed, exact deadline or destination, and hope is tough to articulate when it's a process. They want to know that leadership is making an aggressive attempt to get results. That's where great leaders rise to the challenge.

## Direction

Confidence is key, but communication carries the message and provides clarity. People who follow a leader, as well as other leaders themselves, need clarity because clarity is an explanation of a plan or direction.

But there's a third part of the equation that's imperative—connection. Leaders must connect with their followers. That connection consists of caring with a sincere belief in each other. Connection is not "Give me a chance." It's "I would love for you to succeed." Connection is the emotional feeling people have for each other. It's best described by a word usually avoided in corporate speak for its *scandalous* connotation. The word refers to how we truly, deeply, and emotionally connect with those we lead—our customers and our employees. The word is "intimacy."

Obviously, we're not talking about intimacy in terms of sexual relations. Rather this intimacy is about legitimately caring about someone else, not falsely or for business metrics but for people purposes. This is caring about other people's feelings, their results, and their needs, and it's a fundamental part of connecting.

## World Connections

A great part of my job as CEO of RE/MAX and even before becoming CEO is that I have had the opportunity to meet many great and fascinating people. In fact, I make it a point to learn about the interesting aspects of others, especially the stories people bring to a conversation. You must dig for those stories and sometimes it's slightly uncomfortable. But in doing so you build amazing connections.

Anyone who starts working at RE/MAX must attend Broker 101, an initial training class attended by employees and franchisees together. The weeklong sessions are at our headquarters in Denver, Colorado, and usually include a few dozen people from around the world. Our company has outposts in 110 countries, so we have the privilege of experiencing many different and amazing cultures, perspectives, and people.

One of those fascinating people is Sebastian Sosa, whom I met more than 17 years ago when I went through Broker 101. Sebastian and his wife, Dottie, own the RE/MAX regions of Argentina and Uruguay. We sat in class together along with many others who were then strangers and are now lifelong friends, and we see each several times a year at RE/MAX events around the globe. We stay connected regularly with video calls, too.

How does someone form this kind of lasting long-distance relationship with another? Yes, we trade business, but ultimately it is because we like each other. Here are a few ways to help build your relationships, long-distance and otherwise:

- **Be interested more than interesting.** Everyone likes a good story and wants to hear yours, but don't walk up and start with that. Begin by being genuinely interested in the other person. Ask great questions and care. Remember, no one cares what you know until they know you care.

- **Give freely.** Yes, there it is again. Don't push your business or try to get someone to do something for you. Forming relationships is not a round of speed networking. It's not about seeing who can score the most deals, either. This is about meeting great people. Offer to send the person something that could help them or fascinates them. And do it! No one ever likes a promise that's not kept.

- **Get the person's contact information.** Be able to follow up, and make it easy to do so. I have a QR code on my cell phone's home screen that someone else can shoot a picture of with their phone's camera and instantly have my information. I also always get the person's name, email, and telephone number, then add a note or two about them in my contact list. Usually, emails from individuals contain business information like company websites, too, so be sure to make note. Follow up, and if you have an executive assistant, have that person connect as well with any new contacts and their executive assistants. Introducing the gatekeepers is important to getting things done in the future. Plus, my assistant likes to know who is a genuine contact and who is a vendor randomly reaching out to say, "Hey, I met Adam at an event, and he said to call."

- **Know when to wrap it up.** Don't overstay your welcome. Don't be creepy or awkward. Make the situation valuable, and if it turns into a longer conversation, stick with it but don't do so if it becomes awkward or no one has anything else to say. Move on, but don't forget to take a moment and record your impressions and intentions after the meeting.

- **Follow up!** It's critical, and too many people don't do it. I make it a point to occasionally check in with people I have met and intentionally want to stay in contact with. It doesn't have to be often, but it must be done. If you see something they did on social media or notice something that they are interested in (which is likely something you are interested in as well), send it to them. For those really special situations, an unexpected gift is always a nice touch. But stay in touch.

## SET THE TONE

The modern leader has evolved more than many people realize. They take a holistic approach to being the best person possible and to help others strive for the same thing. It's that leading by example that goes well beyond managing a process.

**Backbone.** Today's leaders give other people the strength to handle their challenges within the process, personally and professionally. Care first; that's how to get things done; that's how to lead, and how to earn the title "leader" every day with your actions.

Most business meetings begin with a problem or challenge, often dealing with employees who are struggling to find the support they need to accomplish a project. Ultimately what those individuals need is the confidence to take action because without it, the Beast—fear—festers. Good leaders don't tell people what to do; they empower them to do it themselves and offer the necessary tools to get started. Then as the employee starts to take action, they discover greater than expected capabilities.

**Direction.** I remember once at a sales meeting I announced a substantial increase in sales quota numbers. When I said that, you could see the fear in the eyes of sales team members. Most sales teams have self-imposed maximum quotas based on peer sales numbers ("How many deals can I make?" for example). Instead, I suggested deconstructing the sales process to gain clarity and then look at how to scale up. It turned out that by building into the process self-imposed accountability and the expectation that each team member makes a certain number of phone calls a day, each salesperson could sell 12 to 20 deals a year as opposed to the eight that had been expected. Once the sales team got over its self-imposed limits, sales results rose to the newly understood capabilities.

The reality is that in sales we are our own worst enemy when it comes to our capabilities because we decide and rationalize downward what we think we can do. That lowered expectation is opposed to what truly can be accomplished when we deconstruct the process and then perform.

Once I was coaching a sales team leader in a different industry. This leader allowed his sales agents to set their own maximum sales cap. For example, his sales agents would visit a client and suggest the normal number of product purchases—perhaps 12. However, they could really sell 40 products to that customer based on the customer's actual needs. So I suggested his teams switch their approach. Instead of saying, "You usually buy 12 products," lead off the sales pitch with "I can typically help 40 people in the office with this product." That slight shift in approach tripled sales, and he became the recognized leader in his organization simply by raising expectations and opportunities.

Don't settle for easy. Party with the Beast and make the most of your efforts. You likely can accomplish much more than you think.

## MORE VARIABLES

Leading also is learning. But learning isn't necessarily leading. It's only one aspect of an equation with many variables. Leading is how you build your learnings into your life and what you do with them as well as the people you associate with and those who influence you. It is having clarity in what you take away from your missions and why, and also being clear about what you give back and why.

---

*"If you are not willing to learn, no one can help you. If you are determined to learn, no one can stop you."*

—Zig Ziglar

---

Learning is as intentional as the intimacy you share with your closest friends and family. It is something that nearly everyone takes for granted. But it is critical. Find the learning people in your life, those who push you to learn.

## ATHLETE ANALOGY

We can compare the similarities of leading by learning to an extreme high-performance athlete. A few of those athletes include Michael Jordan, Tiger Woods, Serena Williams, and Roger Bannister, or Olympians Simone Biles, Usain Bolt, Michael Phelps, and Missy Franklin. Each of them reached the top of their sport, and each practiced strict learning disciplines.

As spectators, we see the results but not all the effort required to obtain the results. We don't see all the moments of learning from others. Those are the minutiae, the tiny adjustments that most people miss because they're only interested rather than hyper-focused on every step in the learning process. Those overlooked details make the difference between good and great.

Leaders train themselves to pay attention to the tiny adjustments and in turn are transparent about sharing those tweaks with others.

---

*When you lead, you influence, so take the role seriously.*

---

## MOST DON'T NOTICE

Most people don't bother to notice what really matters: the details. Years ago my dad, Frank Contos, taught me to get the little things right—the details that pertain to so many aspects of life. He's the same person who taught me to measure twice, cut once.

After all, it's the little things that add up to create overwhelm. Consider the tale of the grasshopper that gets too close to the anthill. The grasshopper is far larger than an ant, and one or even a few ants don't make any difference to it. But when the grasshopper gets overwhelmed by the ant colony, it can't move and dies where it stands.

The same concept applies to life. Take care of the little things as you encounter them so they don't add up to overwhelm. The same goes for your equipment in life. In the military, it's the gear needed to do your job. In law enforcement, too, there's plenty of equipment that you rely on to protect your life and the lives of others. If it's in disrepair and disorganized, it will fail or will be unavailable when needed to save a life. Don't neglect what can save you.

People tend to look at leaders as having accomplished great things. Yet when you're asked to recall some of those accomplishments, you can't think of any. That's because any great accomplishment is the culmination of many small efforts and countless trials and tribulations, much thought, and serious research.

We tend to be a one and done society—we look to either blame or brag about one thing in someone's life, one accomplishment by a leader, one action on which to judge. Consider Steve Jobs of Apple fame. Is the iPhone his great accomplishment? Or is it the Mac computer? Or what about his efforts to make computing beautiful or perhaps to create iTunes? While all those are great accomplishments, what we don't think about are all the small steps he took. Jobs was relentless in the small efforts of perfection.

## LITTLE BITS ADD UP

Life must be maintained, or it gets expensive. Leadership must be maintained, too. The little things needed to maintain leadership are easy if you do them daily. But they become progressively harder if you don't. Leadership expert Jim Rohn says that we suffer two kinds of psychological pain in life: the pain of discipline and the pain of regret. The pain of discipline weighs ounces, while the pain of regret weighs tons.

Discipline is doing the little things each day, from watching your diet and health to keeping tabs on relationships, business, finances, happiness, and belongings. The pain of regret is when you don't maintain those aspects of your life and suddenly discover that they have been neglected so badly that they are often beyond salvaging.

Darren Hardy, author of *The Compound Effect*, says it best: Life success and leadership success are just doing the little things well that others put off.

Details have always mattered in my life. My leadership has evolved but the details are the foundation, the life choices. Each of us has the ability to focus on making decisions if we keep the clutter out and clarity in. It's easy to let tiny things slide, but they add to the confusion and the distractions in crisis. When we keep things around us sorted, our mind is sorted so that when chaos enters the scene the path to calm is more direct. If we are in chaos and more chaos comes our way, it's just more chaos to contend with. Keep up with the details. (More on coping with chaos in the next chapter.)

## WAKE UP AND LEARN

Many people go through life with their heads down, doing what they think they need to do to survive. We've all likely gone through an iteration of this at some point in our lives, in some job we didn't like as a teenager, for example, even if it was just mowing the lawn or shoveling snow.

Other people jump into a situation or a job headfirst. Unfortunately, that doesn't always mean they come away any wiser. There are a select few, though, who find moments of awakening and walk away with a vulnerable realization that they can truly become better with the associations they build and the efforts they put into those associations.

Real leaders experience many of these awakenings throughout their careers. Sometimes leaders deliberately inject themselves into these learning situations. Other times they end up in the middle as part of a meeting, event, chance conversation, job review, or even sitting at dinner with friends and diving into the day's thoughts or experiences. The reality is that we must make these opportunities as intentional as possible to truly aim for the win to lead and learn. Relaxed conversation is as important—sometimes more so—than intentional agenda-based conversation because free-flowing thoughts can develop and brilliance emerge.

These situations only reinforce the importance of a hyper-awareness of learning. I think of it as a superpower that can be developed and deployed like sunshine. When that sunshine is focused off of a mirror, it's intense. But without the mirror, it's only sunshine that we take for granted every day.

When you intentionally and deeply focus on learning, you often cultivate a sense of leadership Zen, and your mind truly grows through thought. That's leading by learning. That's growing and changing and getting better.

Continue to change; change often and change a lot. Learn to be comfortable with change, too, because change is good—especially when it's you who changes. And find those people around you who can help you change.

When I left the Douglas County (Colorado) Sheriff's Office to go into the corporate world, a few people said to me, "Don't make the change." I asked, "Why not?" Isn't the point of change to get better so I can help more people?" With that statement, the doubters saw the opportunity and agreed. Change is good if it's used for good. Those people who don't want you to change are the monkeys keeping you from climbing the ladder and reaching the banana.

## THE GOAL: REPLACE YOURSELF

The real job of a leader is to build other great leaders—to work themselves out of a job. That's right—find someone better and smarter to replace you. As leaders we work to give our jobs away to someone we have developed to be better than we are.

Leaders must discover potential in others, encourage that potential, and help to build it so much that the leader becomes obsolete. Then the leader can excitedly step aside, yielding to the next generation.

Unfortunately, leaders with egos feel threatened and often hoard their power rather than relinquish it. Those egomaniacs think they're the smartest person in the room and irreplaceable. The reality, though, is that they should be replaced immediately.

In building new leaders, old leaders step aside with satisfaction to watch their creations succeed. Just as Michelangelo saw the potential in his block of marble and then sculpted his great statue *David* over several years, a leader must have the patience to see the potential in someone else.

Great things come from humble beginnings. At some point as a leader, you must move on to allow your creations to stand on their own.

# FAILURE

People are fascinated by failures of successful people, not only to know how and why they failed, but also how they recovered and rebounded.

## Normal Occurrence

First, we have all failed at something. I've failed many times. Failure is a normal part of my life, and I'm OK with that. Lots of things don't go right the first time, but I learn from those mistakes, face the changes or consequences, and move past them. We can't dwell on what we did wrong or beat ourselves up over a mistake. Instead, accept the situation and move on.

When we learn from the missteps and move on quickly, people sometimes interpret that to mean we don't care about our screwups. But the reality is that someone who makes a mistake and moves on has the grace and humility to admit it, to care about it, and to keep going. Earlier I talked about basketball great Michael Jordan. He's failed a lot, but not many people realize that because he has succeeded a great deal, too. Consider these telling words from Jordan that are repeated again and again as inspiration:

*I have missed more than 9,000 shots in my career. I have lost almost 300 games and on 26 occasions I was able to make the basket that won the game and I missed. I have failed over and over again in my life. And for that reason, I have succeeded.*[1]

## Forget the Blame Game

Failure is not about blame, either. It is about which part of the framework did not work based on expectations. Too often society prefers to point the finger of blame. That's not what great leaders do.

Rather, they give themselves and others grace while identifying the breakdown in the framework and learning. No one is so great at everything that they have the right to condemn others. Those who do are narcissistic, egotistical, and emotionally immature.

When someone screws up, deal with it or allow that person to deal with it and move on.

The people you want in your life are the ones with the best of intentions, not those who hide their intentions. It's OK to make mistakes; it's not OK to blame your mistakes on others. It's also not OK to browbeat or belittle others for their mistakes. Instead ask, "What can we do differently next time?" or "What's the very best way we can accomplish this?" Life is about making mistakes. Without mistakes we wouldn't have many great inventions. A few examples include:

- Penicillin: Its discoverer, Alexander Fleming, forgot to clean a petri dish before he took a trip in 1928. When he returned, he

---

[1]Michael Jordan, "Failure," February 16, 2012 (accessed May 1, 2021), https://www.youtube.com/watch?v=GuXZFQKKF7A.

noticed mold had formed on the dish and prevented the spread of bacteria.[2]

- Post–it Notes: Spencer Silver, a scientist at 3M, tried to develop a super-strong adhesive. Instead, he created such a weak adhesive that it could be easily lifted off a surface, and the precursor to Post–it Notes was born.[3]

- Cardiac pacemaker: U.S. engineer and inventor Wilson Greatbatch was trying to create a heart rhythm recording device in 1958, when he mistakenly installed the wrong part. He noticed a small steady electric pulse coming from the device, and that led to the first implantable cardiac pacemaker.[4]

Admittedly, not all failures turn into giant successes. Many are dead ends. That's OK, though. We simply must keep trying.

## The Best of Plans. . .

One day my team brought me what seemed like a great business deal. I was excited, too, because it would help my customers and those with whom I do business. We worked hard to set up the relationship, build a plan, and start with a great launch.

However, when we launched, our partner's actions suddenly shifted gears and were far less appealing. Plenty of pushback ensued, and we eventually parted ways with the new partners. Naturally, I

---

[2]Robert Gaynes, "The Discovery of Penicillin: New Insights After More than 75 Years of Clinical Use," *Emerging Infectious Diseases* (May 2017): 23–5, 8490853 (accessed May 1, 2021), 849–853 DOI, 10.3201/eid2305.161556, PMCID: PMC5403050U.S. National Library of Medicine, National Institutes of Health, http://dx.doi.org/10.3201/eid2305.161556; https://www.ncbi.nlm.nih.gov/pmc/articles/PMC5403050/.

[3]Post-it® Brand, History Timeline: Post-it® Notes (accessed May 1, 2021), https://www.post-it.com/3M/en_US/post-it/contact-us/about-us/.

[4]Lemelson-MIT, "Wilson Greatbatch: Invented a Device that Emitted Electronic Pulses to the Heart," Massachusetts Institute of Technology (accessed May 15, 2021), https://lemelson.mit.edu/award-winners/wilson-greatbatch.

received numerous complaints about the deal even though we had the best of intentions and had done our due diligence to minimize any anticipated roadblocks (risks).

Unfortunately, we couldn't plan for the unforeseen. So when our new partners started to operate in a manner contrary to our ideals and with our reputation on the line, we pulled out of the deal. We could do that because we are values-driven, not ego-driven like many other companies and their leaders. Those impacted understood. Others second-guessed as to why we did what we did. But we knew it was the right thing to do, and we moved on, our pride of excellence intact.

Some people may think my calm response to the deal's failure was too laid back. But the reality is that the strongest leaders typically exert the least amount of force to correct issues with their teams. We adjust frameworks for processes because the teams hold themselves to such a high level that all a leader must do is pick them up and redeploy resources.

If a team handles its failures properly, the right people fix themselves. Failing isn't easy or fun. But strong teams realize where they are weak or incapable and diligently seek to improve. The leader simply supplies the oversight to accomplish the improvements. Great teams have great humility because of their humble leaders.

## COPING WITH FAILURE

How do we get to a point where we are OK with failure and excited to try again? The answers are in the learning.

Recently, my wife and I vacationed with friends, one of whom fished every day. The first day our friend returned from fishing so excited that we assumed he had caught a giant bonefish, so we asked, "What did you catch?"

Surprisingly, he said, "Nothing." And of course, we offered our condolences. But his reply was amazing. He said his day was awesome because he had learned so much and had a great time learning. What a great attitude!

The next day, bright and early, our friend headed out again. That afternoon he returned sunburned, tired, and with a huge smile. We asked, "What did you catch today?"

Again, his answer surprised us: "Didn't catch anything, but I learned a lot more today." The third, fourth, and fifth days of fishing netted the same responses. By the sixth day, we were talking about what he had learned about fishing each day, not about his lack of a catch.

Our friend didn't see his inability to catch a fish as failure. He was excited about all that he learned in trying, not in accomplishing. He was in love with the process, not the results. I have learned that true leaders have a deep appreciation for the process and how they can learn from it every day.

That's why, as our fishless fisherman friend so aptly demonstrates, it's so important as a leader never to stop building on your learnings.

# THE POWER OF HOW WE LEARN

It's not so much what you learn as it is how you learn. Take a minute to consider that. Break down your habits; consider how you process inputs, what you do with the information, and how you apply it to create outputs. Think about it in terms of business, school, life, relationships, and more.

## Environments Matter

When you create a great environment and habit for how you learn, you actually magnify what you learn. It's like exercising. When you go to the gym or even exercise at home, do you go through the motions, or are you making the absolute most of the time and the exercise? Is it a social hour at the gym, or is it exercise? The goal, of course, should be to take every effort and motion seriously with hyper-focus on the most results possible.

It should be the same when it comes to learning. Be intentional and hyper-focused on getting the most possible out of a mission, a learning experience. The learning process and framework for creating a successful learning environment are as important as the content. When you create an amazing learning environment, what you learn becomes more effective. This is the genesis for higher education and business growth.

## Habits Make the Difference

Few people recognize that the work-life habits you create as a young adult in college and graduate school shape your business and relationship habits throughout life. Even if you didn't attend college or did but didn't develop good learning skills, if you create a daily system for winning and learning, you create growth in your life.

In fact, that's a secret for massive success. We each must establish personal learning systems and habits to help break down the overwhelming amount of information we throw at ourselves each day. When we do that, the learnings become more valuable and longer lasting. It's back to breaking down challenges into manageable pieces and then digesting them one at a time.

Our youngest daughter, Maggie, just finished her freshman year of college. Even though most freshmen struggle (nearly one-third drop out their first year[5]), Maggie had an amazing year because she understood how to approach this huge challenge. She broke it down into small systems, which, when executed consistently, create great results. She was happy because she was organized and systematic in her efforts. She carried a full class load—more than many of her peers—but earned top grades due to her organizational skills.

Maggie keeps a daily planning journal every day on her iPad, documenting what has to be done, when, and recording when it is accomplished. She also takes advantage of the 24 hours in the day to maintain her health, nutrition, and happiness, yet still manages to get all of her work done before it is due and with a lower level of stress than her peers. Why? Because Maggie has developed intentional habits that make the difference.

---

[5]Educationdata.org, "General Statistics: College Dropout Rates" (accessed May 16, 2021), https://educationdata.org/college-dropout-rates.

## TAKE THE TIME

So how do all of these items play together in winning and leadership? They all work only if you work them.

Life is intentional. So is learning. Too many people spin through life to "get it done." That's great, but did they actually create impact? Did they put in the effort to create great results? Did they "measure twice and cut once"? Do it right, and the habits become results.

One of the tenets of our SWAT team was excellence—in what we did and how we did it. A great example was at the shooting range. Unfortunately, police officers sometimes must fire their weapons in the line of duty to stop a threat or imminent threat of another person causing death or serious bodily injury. It's a last-ditch effort that must be as precise as practically possible during a generally chaotic situation.

SWAT officers, especially, are expected to be tops in all aspects of the job, including operating firearms, if necessary. That means being precise in how you engage a threat or, on the firing range for practice, on how you engage a target.

When a police officer fires their weapon, they are responsible for where that bullet goes. If the bullet misses its intended target and hits an innocent person, that's a horrible fail. If the bullet misses its intended target, and that person causes more hurt and harm as a result, that's not the intended outcome, either.

## HUGE RESPONSIBILITY

The capacity to use lethal force is a heavy responsibility for a law enforcement officer. Society has placed a huge trust in these officers to make this ultimate decision of life or death and carry out the actions surrounding it.

Precise, perfect practice and extensive training is a necessity. That's why as SWAT officers we focused heavily on these skills and practiced them regularly. Excellence was and is always the goal. To achieve that means repetition of the basics. That's right, a team of experts working on the basics. As a SWAT officer, I worked on the exact same skills taught to new shooters—over and over again.

Why? Because these basics are what most people get wrong. Too often we feel we are beyond the basics, and as a result our skills creep away to easy instead of precise. It's the basics of anything that matters. Before his auto accident, golfer Tiger Woods made hundreds of putts every day. Basketball great Michael Jordan would stand at the free-throw line and shoot free throws one after another. Tennis mastermind Serena Williams has a serve of more than 128 miles per hour, yet she practices and practices and practices it.

## MORE OF THE BASICS

Practicing and studying and learning and relearning the basics over and over again is why winning and leadership aren't exciting. They're not glamorous or interesting, either. They are about the basics, perfected through the daily effort of making them work.

However, once you create the habit of the basics each day, you learn to perfect everything from making your bed when you wake up to greeting people. You apply the learnings, whether they are the learnings related to being a good dog or pet owner, exercising and eating healthy, or making the most of a business process or transaction.

It is a basic framework that works. And the basics become habits. Practice, practice, and more practice is incredibly important because under stress we operate at the level of our training. I learned that back in my days in law enforcement. When I encountered that felony in progress as a rookie cop in the megachurch sanctuary in Colorado, I was scared while looking for that burglar, but I had practiced and practiced how to apprehend an armed suspect. So when faced with the situation, I acted instinctively based on my training.

How you train is how you will perform in actual situations, whether it's a police operation, a high-level SWAT mission, or networking at a business event. Almost all of us in whatever we do have some type of continuing training or education requirement.

As a police officer, I had to spend hours practicing how to put handcuffs on would-be suspects because those individuals spend many hours training to get away from the police. Cops spend hours practicing driving their patrol cars in reverse, too. Why? Because most police accidents occur while driving with cruisers in reverse. Similarly, attorneys, accountants, real estate agents, teachers, and more all spend time practicing and pursuing how to be better at their jobs.

Remember, it's the little things done right and practiced each day that make the difference. Compounded, they become leadership and daily wins.

## STAY HUNGRY, STAY HUMBLE

I enjoy leading, both the aspect of being the instructor and of helping others. Yet I also enjoy being a student, a beginner with a learning mind. Recognizing that in a mastermind session was a real wake-up call.

We were sitting as a small group, talking to the CEO of one of the largest software companies in the world. The man is one of those leaders you look at and instantly understand why he is where he is. He's truly gifted and extremely humble—something each of us should aspire to emulate.

He asked if we had any questions for him. I told him that I hoped to be the greatest CEO I possibly could, and asked if he had any advice. Instantly this leader had the answer. "It's simple but very complex," he said. "Stay hungry; stay humble."

Then he paused meaningfully as if to allow that wisdom to soak in. When he was sure we had digested its simple genius, he moved on. It was now on me to unpack what those four words really meant. To this day, I have a sign in my office that says: "Stay hungry, stay humble." My perspective is if you lose either your hunger or your humility, you lose, period.

# LEADING FOR A WIN

One night while still in law enforcement, I was on a call involving a possibly angry and intoxicated male wandering aimlessly around a business district yelling at people. This type of call is common; many involve mental health issues, and law enforcement is called in to resolve the situation to ensure peace and protection of the public as well as to ensure the person is not a threat to themselves or others.

In my experience, the best way to deal with an unstable or emotionally charged situation is to be respectful of the individual and try to help—show up, meet them, understand their challenges, earn their trust and confidence, and help them. Everybody wins.

Another officer showed up on the scene, too. He was confident and capable, former military and a martial artist. We found the man walking around yelling and waving his arms, so trying a friendly approach, we said, "Hey man, what's going on?" The man was angry that we were on the scene, and that immediately sent his tension level up a notch.

But then we followed up with a few words that took him off guard: "What can I help you with?" It was an open-ended question and different from the typical, "Can I help you with anything?" The latter usually elicits a negative response followed by "You can leave." Undaunted, though, your next reply is, "Let's figure out some ways to make your day better."

# GIVE, GIVE, GIVE

All of these are giving statements. People, no matter who they are or their circumstances, appreciate giving. They like compliments, too—perhaps "Hey, cool shoes" or "I like that watch; what is it?" Remember the two things we can't give ourselves—personal attention and appreciation.

As law enforcement, we were trying to break the ice and establish a rapport with this very distraught man without inciting negativity and defensiveness. Another way we could have done that would be to avoid questions with the accusatory word "why." Also, it's important to have fun and enjoy talking with people. Fun eases tensions and can draw others into the conversation. Some think that may be unprofessional; I call it effective. I have watched officers dance in contests, toss around a football, shoot hoops, or even skateboard with kids.

It turned out that our distraught wanderer was angry about something that had happened at his work. Unsure of how to blow off steam, he had gotten off the bus at an unfamiliar stop. That sort of thing happens all the time; people end up in an undesirable location due to the unforeseen challenges they face. Many end up in jail for being angry and committing a crime out of emotions instead of talking to someone to help them.

## POWER OF UNDERSTANDING

We were able to get this man to talk to us, and we all ended up laughing together over cups of coffee. All ended well simply because we were kind and respectful. We understood his frustration and helped him with it. He simply needed to understand what was going on and be OK with himself. While not all calls end up like this, it's an example of flipping the paradigm of anger to one of understanding.

From a scientific standpoint, these needs relate to Abraham Maslow's theory of human motivation, commonly known as Maslow's hierarchy of needs. An American psychologist, Maslow first proposed his theory in an article for *Psychological Review* that appeared in 1943.

The basic premise is that we all have human needs that must be met one at a time and in a specific order so that we can achieve our goal of self-actualization—to be happy, safe, and proud of ourselves.[6]

---

[6]A.H. Maslow, "A Theory of Human Motivation," *Psychological Review* 50 (1943): 370–96 (accessed May 1, 2021), https://citeseerx.ist.psu.edu/viewdoc/summary?doi=10.1.1.334.7586; http://psychclassics.yorku.ca/Maslow/motivation.htm.

## AVOID BATTLE

The same goes in business. Kindness and respect set the stage for wins. To fully understand how employees, customers, and those you lead think, know that everyone wants to feel safe.

Imagine this scenario: You're having an argument with your spouse or partner and someone calls the police. The police arrive, and now the officer becomes the "bad guy" and all the officer did was respond to a radio call to help figure out someone's challenge.

Or maybe instead of the argument with your at-home partner, it's a disagreement over a contract with a business partner. One side immediately finds itself at odds with the other, so both sides cast aside all past relationships in favor of a battle for the win. What happened? How do we stop the snowball effect of creating an emotional avalanche?

## REALITY CHECK

First, people—in business and in life—make mistakes. Nothing in life is perfect, and if you expect perfection you face constant disappointment. (Note: Disappointment is a choice you make.) Instead, notice and don't judge. Noticing is an act; judging is an emotion.

No matter what, in business, as a customer, in observing and dealing with your children's schools, or even in traffic, remember that nothing is perfect. Don't allow that expectation of perfection to overshadow reality.

Nonetheless, most less-than-ideal situations are the result of an accident or some unintentional statement or action. People typically have good intentions; we just aren't perfect. Get over it and move on. The bottom line is that confrontations are a junction of frustration and anger, and it takes a reverse course to create a beneficial outcome.

Here's a good way to judge satisfaction levels—whether it's satisfaction with action, performance, or even a person. How close is it to your version of perfect? Was it between minimally acceptable and perfect? Or did you initially set unrealistic expectations and find disappointment by saying, "I wish it could have been. . ." Don't set yourself up for lifelong disappointment. When someone gives their best and it isn't to your liking, go somewhere else to find another option. But don't expect everyone to live by your rules when from the beginning you likely didn't perform for others at a high level.

## TAME THE BEAST

When you're frustrated or angry, you are automatically the loser, period. When the Beast rears its head, you're easily manipulated by the situation or someone else in the situation, or you fight back. The magical solution, as I learned as a police officer and shared above, is to say, "Thank you," offer love and respect, provide dignity, and act with grace.

Being a better person almost always solves the problem. Use those words mentioned above in the situation and be genuinely caring in how you deploy them. Giving grace is good for the win, even if it doesn't initially feel like it. The better person may take a few impacts in the process—financially or egotistically—because of their kindness, especially from people filled with rage and hate. But the reality is that nothing can make some people happy or even content. When you talk to people, tell them you want to give them dignity, grace, and respect in how you do anything and everything. Also let them know that you are kind and love their passion for their efforts, and especially their feelings about the situation.

This is a respectful acknowledgment of someone as a person; people want that. Be genuine, but don't allow someone to run excuses around your statements. Simply say, "Thank you" and then, "This is how we will move forward."

## HANDLING THE TOUGH

Probably the toughest job as a leader is to fire someone. And it should be tough because great leaders care about other people—the person being let go, their family, and their ego. First and foremost, the right way to fire an employee is to let them go with dignity and grace even when they are acting otherwise.

Each of us hopes never to have to fire someone. It's natural not to want to have a massive, negative impact on someone's life. But faced with a situation that requires a dismissal, we have to think about whether the impact is truly negative or whether in the long run we are helping that individual get control of their life. That may sound cruel, but each of us needs an occasional wake-up call and a realignment in our lives and businesses.

Unfortunately, though, no matter how good our intentions or how right something is for all involved, the person being let go likely will not see it or feel it in the moment. I have had people hug me on their way out the door, and I've also had people leave the business in handcuffs for breaking the law and being fired for it. Either way, you need to be the best, kindest leader possible because everyone else is watching how you handle this.

No matter the situation, the person walking out the door is going to leave a little bruised, even if only temporarily. Sometimes it's hard to see that the hurt is temporary because as their leader, it hurts me too. After all, this is life, and life is not just a business transaction.

# BANK ACCOUNT OF LIFE

Sorry to be the bearer of bad news. But if each of us doesn't try to get better every day, if we aren't always growing and learning, then we're actually getting worse. That's because nothing stays the same. Days that go by without personal growth are days lost.

## Deposits Add Up

Think of life as a big bank account; we make new deposits (new learnings) every day. We make big withdrawals, too, with one misstep, one failed action, or one missed opportunity. Unfortunately, it's not a one-for-one comparison. If we screw up and withdraw from our account, we can't make up for it with one positive day or one winning mission.

The same thing happens with your health. Every day that you eat healthy, exercise, and hydrate adds up. But if one day you eat junk, sit on the couch, and avoid drinking water, that adds up, too, to an unhealthy lifestyle. Again, it's not a one-for-one comparison. Losses take more of toll than gains provide.

## . . .So Do Withdrawals

Life is not equal in terms of effort and results. Just as in a business relationship, if you seriously insult someone, the harm done cannot be undone by simply being nice the next day. The relationship must be re-earned; sometimes we even must start over.

At times in the course of doing business, you may totally cash out your account—encounter an epic fail, for example—and may have to start fresh. That's why it's so important not to let a day go by without learning, without growing, and without getting better. Even that epic fail can be a learning experience.

# DON'T MISS AN OPPORTUNITY

Growth in leadership works the same way. Learning is not equal in terms of effort to results. We must work harder and do more to grow as leaders—far more. So, it's important to focus on a multitude of opportunities each day. We must learn to live a growth lifestyle by building leadership and growth habits into our everyday lives.

I've built growth habits into my daily life since I was a teenager. It wasn't difficult to get up each day whether I was going out to play or headed to work because I was always excited about something. Life then and now isn't about hiding from the day; it's about finding the opportunities in the day. As a result, I always had a job, or school, or some responsibility. When I was a kid, my jobs ranged from washing dishes at a breakfast restaurant called Country Kitchen to pumping gas and scooping frozen yogurt.

My dad taught me that my work ethic and effort were what would get me anywhere, so I invested the effort into always doing the very best job possible and paying attention to the details. That's when I discovered that leadership doesn't come from others; it comes from within when you lead yourself to demonstrate leadership to others. You can't successfully tell someone what to do or they will despise you. Instead, you must do it yourself and show them what to do; you learn so they learn; you're present so they are present. It's you living a leadership life so others see this and want to do the same.

No one can just walk up to you and give you the ability to have positive habits. If you don't have accountability in your life, you won't have habits. You can learn accountability by yourself or with a coach, trainer, or spouse/partner who helps you stay on the commitment track. Plenty of great books are written about accountability, too, that help you understand how habits and consistency build small movements to get better incrementally.

Most businesses and organizations work on a daily management basis with their employees to bolster habits and consistency. When I first met Dave Liniger, like so many others, he recommended books to help push the philosophy of personal growth. While traveling with Dave during our time together at RE/MAX, we gave speaking tours as part of educational programs for our brokers and agents. When we traveled, we read new business and personal development books and compared notes every night. It was an amazing growth experience, and we still do this on a friendly basis since his retirement from the company. (He is still chairman of the board.)

More recently, I've had the opportunity to do this with my family. My kids, Jack, Ashleigh, and Maggie, and wife, Kelly, are interested in how to be the best they can be. Evenings after dinner when they are all home from school, we sit around the backyard fire pit, roast s'mores, and hold our own book club, talking about books like *Atomic Habits* by James Clear. I have read this book several times, but the reality was that revisiting the concepts under current circumstances was a great study in applying the philosophies to current challenges. Everyone learned a great deal about themselves. We were vulnerable in the discussions and have since applied new frameworks for success as we discussed from the book. This is leadership.

While I've had coaches, mentors, and mastermind memberships, and continue to do so, building winning principles into my life has become easier since my family has become engaged in doing so as well. When we discuss the concepts more frequently, we have fewer struggles than when we let time pass without reviewing them. The human mind wanders to a framework-less approach when you allow it—discipline takes effort, as author Jocko Willink says in his book *Discipline Equals Freedom*. My family continues to push each other on these concepts, just as I had to push myself decades ago when breaking into leadership. It is a daily effort but brings daily rewards.

## IRRITANT OR LEADERSHIP COURSE?

A few of the above suggestions may sound a bit annoying to some, but to others on the leadership path, this way of living life to the fullest can be very rewarding. When you do these things every day, they eventually become habit—routines repeated automatically and without resistance. For example, I get up at 4:30 a.m. five days a week to head to the gym. Admittedly it's a bit early and it's not the most enjoyable way to spend an hour, but it's a great contributor to physical and mental health and, as a result, to business health, too. (I sleep in until 5:30 a.m. the other days before going out to exercise.)

Wouldn't you like to go to sleep every night satisfied that it's been a good day, that whether it included a win or a learning, you've done everything you could to grow, learn, and improve at what you do? Wouldn't you like to wake up refreshed and excited every morning for the new opportunity to grow and learn? You can wake up eager in the morning and go to sleep satisfied at night if you commit to starting every day with a win. (Some great reading on this comes from Darren Hardy, in his book *The Compound Effect*.)

Getting on track toward wins as a leader and a person is up to you. It's back to the locus of control: You and your actions, or lack thereof, determine the direction of your life.

## It's Up to You

You are the bank that holds these accounts and these habits. You are the catalyst for growth or loss. Too often the choice is to blame others or the environment—as in a poor economy—for the missteps and inactions in life. But the reality is that it's up to you.

Think about what happens when an employee or, worse yet, a leader offends a customer. Perhaps that person used poor word choice and insulted someone, or an order was seriously off the mark, or there was a misunderstanding of some kind. Saying, "I'm sorry; it won't happen again" generally isn't enough to win back the customer's loyalty. More likely, it takes discounts, hand-holding, and multiple apologies at the very least to atone for the faux pas. It shouldn't, though, as someone with grace would simply say, "That's OK; things happen." Unfortunately, too many people in today's society seem to want you to pay a penance to them for an innocent mistake.

To repeat, it's back to locus of control. Take responsibility for your learning and your leadership. Seek out leaders, and you'll find them—sometimes when you don't expect to. If you don't take the initiative, you won't see these people leading, and thus you won't learn from them.

# LOOK FOR LEADERS

Leaders use a calculated and educated perspective to observe and then take the right chances. When we actively look for leaders, go out of our way to learn their philosophies, pay attention to their trials and tribulations, and emulate what works for them, we each become a better problem-solver and more impactful leader.

Pay attention, too, to how leaders interact with others, their emotions, responses, and tactics. They offer even more insight into how you can grow and improve your own leadership skills.

A great way to learn leadership—even if it's what not to do—is to watch how a leader handles the situation when an employee has a question or problem. I was watching a business meeting—an outsider looking in—in which employees were asking the leader questions. One employee asked something that clearly disturbed the leader, and he in turn demeaned the employee publicly.

The situation was terrible. The egotistical manager obviously felt he could bark orders, demand performance, and belittle another human being. This was not leadership. It was a sorry situation that gives management everywhere a bad name.

This manager's behavior also was a reflection on the company and the other managers who tolerated it. Now all of them had to deal with the situation because of one person's ego. This manager should have used the simple principle of praise in public, criticize in private—if criticism is even necessary. The reality is that this employee spoke out because he thought he had a valid question for the manager. The manager's misuse of the question-and-answer podium not only hurt this employee, but also changed everyone's impression of what is allowed as leadership in the company.

The incident also prompted a realization for me: I don't ever want to work for a jerk. Jerks aren't leaders, and leaders aren't jerks.

## WARNING SIGNS OF CRUMBLING LEADERSHIP

Equally as important as what leaders do right is what they do wrong. We always hear when leaders succeed or masterfully fail, but what about when they start to crumble, when little nuances indicate "the wall is cracked"?

## Subtle Signs

Often, the signs are subtle or gradual and usually relate to aspects of a leader's life other than business. Perhaps their relationship integrity, ethics, or honesty is slipping. Maybe the leader becomes hypocritical in what they say or do in their personal time compared with what they espouse in their business life. Perhaps a leader cheats on a spouse or significant other. Remember, we are what we repeatedly do.

Every collapsing leader crumbles just as they succeeded, in their own unique way. Try this exercise: Watch when someone falls out of the leadership pack and ask yourself why. What did that person do or not do? What did they say? What exposed their weaknesses as a human being—and what were those weaknesses?

We each can learn from watching other leaders regardless of the industry (that's what masterminds are all about—more on that later). Observing leaders is important, too, because those you lead are watching the same things you are—and assessing your strengths and weaknesses.

## Toxicity Can Spread

One of the biggest cracks in the wall—a leadership failure—that can easily crumble an organization is a toxic employee who management won't terminate. We've all crossed paths with someone like that—disruptive, negative, self-serving, and often even hostile. Worse, these toxic employees are personally miserable and, like a virus, spread negativity.

**Quick response essential.** Too often, companies and their leaders don't act fast enough to fire the employee—solve the problem—out of fear. Companies have collapsed because of that failure to take action. The crack in the wall of your business must be fixed quickly or the wall will come down.

---

*"An employee will cost you the most between when you think they should leave your company and when they actually do."*

—Darren Hardy, author, success mentor (www.darrenhardy.com)

---

When you encounter negative people, try exuding kindness. I've found that the nicer and calmer I am, the more a negative person reveals their true intentions, which eventually leads to their own demise. It's like a chess game—your move, their move, and then figure out the reasons behind the move.

Be kind and give that person an opportunity to change, then measure their response to your feedback—understand and respond but be ready to act swiftly. I am quick to recognize the negative, and I'm just as quick to get away from it if I don't see a use for it. Keep in mind, too, that your response affects others' feelings and their negativity or positivity.

**Model the values up front.** Better still, to avoid the problem altogether, leaders need to model their values and be present in their organization. When the leader's values are on full display, someone who doesn't share similar values will recognize they're not welcome in that organization and won't join it. That's one reason many companies today work so diligently at recruiting team members who match a company's culture.

**Not a team player.** I remember a co-worker I supervised who was self-centered and not team-oriented. I offered them very clear and kind advice on what I wanted to see and how they could reshape their leadership and growth. A few weeks went by and nothing changed. They decided that they didn't want to be a part of our championship quality team, and instead wanted to be an all-star individual player.

They were quickly moved to pursue their goal of excellence elsewhere. They had no desire to be part of the team; they were in it for themselves, not the team, so they were cut from the team. Interestingly, the team soared as soon as this person left. You may encounter criticism from those outside the situation looking in. However, that usually means you will also win praise from people within the situation directly affected by this negative, self-serving person.

Don't dwell on the situation any longer; quickly move on to new successes. You helped the team by helping someone who was struggling—the banished team member—and you help the customers who reap the rewards of the new excellence of the team serving them.

When you fail to act to remove the bad apple, you end up losing many of the right people instead of letting the one wrong person go.

# LEADER MORE THAN INSTRUCTOR

When I made that felony collar as a rookie cop, my teacher with me at the time was the shift sergeant, Pat. She was an amazing teacher, an incredibly strong leader, and a great role model. Pat taught me practical application of the fundamentals I had learned in the police academy and the professionalism that only on-the-job training offers.

Pat would debrief me, and we would talk about learning principles. She was a leader who shared knowledge, not an instructor who handed out bullet points. Back then my small police department recognized that we can all learn from everyone, period, and everyone should have a chance to share their knowledge.

# BEYOND TEACHING

Like Pat, a great teacher is also a great leader. They don't provide verbatim instruction. Rather, they influence the formation of knowledge through understanding and perspective. Pat encouraged me to want to do my best.

How much you want to achieve something trumps knowing how to do something. That's because if you have the desire to accomplish something, you always will figure out how to get it done. That includes tapping into outside resources, working tirelessly, and making adjustments without ego.

Not everyone believes enough in themselves to lead, but anyone can be a leader if they seize the opportunity and capitalize on it. True leaders understand the value of inclusivity in all that they do. They know how to embrace vulnerability, too.

As I learned as a cop early on, great leaders don't demand their people to take stands on social issues. Instead, they demonstrate the desired behavior. When people see their leaders' actions, they mimic those actions.

## ACTIONS, NOT JUST WORDS

The RE/MAX statement of inclusivity is "Do the right thing." Leaders are quick to respond, and that response must be one of kindness regardless of the circumstances or people involved. It must be a demonstration of dignity and equality and illustrate our leadership in society. Does your value statement reflect that leadership?

RE/MAX's position has always been inclusive in all aspects of our operations. We abide by fair housing rules and believe in fair and equal treatment of everyone. When I took over as CEO, my team and I decided we wanted to update our values statement because it's something we are proud of as an organization and we live up to the standards every day. We have regular meetings, too, to discuss our values and keep them top of mind. A company's values are the North Star for the organization's direction.

We simplified and personalized our values to the acronym MORE. Are you living MORE? Are you doing that project with MORE? How do we make this MORE? We use it regularly around our business, and I am publicly proud of it. MORE stands for:

* Deliver to the Max.
* Be customer Obsessed.
* Do the Right thing.
* Together Everybody wins.

# THE POWER OF VULNERABILITY

Have you ever seen a leader cry? What about a winner or someone you put on a pedestal? I have, and I have cried as a result of my leadership, too. Feelings are part of the human condition. Leaders lead people and need to care. Those who don't care aren't leaders.

## All About Emotions

Vulnerability is giving away control of your emotions to others. Others can harm your emotions if you allow it, by sharing personal problems, for example.

Vulnerable is a buzzword these days; so many leaders say that they're being vulnerable, but they truly don't know how to be. The only real way to know you are willing to be vulnerable is to ask, "Do people trust you with their emotions?" Because if you trust them with yours, they will likely reciprocate and bring you their challenges as well.

But in order to do that, your people also must know that you face challenges, too. My wife, Kelly, and I have been through various struggles with our children. We've had our parenting abilities challenged. We have both been through divorces and custody battles, and the emotional process of me adopting her children. We have had close friends fight addiction and others who have faced depression and dealt with suicide.

Life throws us many curveballs. Leaders get the same number of at-bats as everyone else. Don't hide from your issues; you will discover that when you are vulnerable and transparent as a person and a leader, you will understand that there are many people out there who will step up to share their struggles to get your perspective . . . and offer their love to help you with yours.

## Humanity

I was on a business trip a few years ago and had just boarded my plane bound for Denver from Florida's west coast. I sat down next to an older woman; we'll call her Louise. She had preboarded in a wheelchair. We both smiled at each other. She was frail and sweet—you could see it in her eyes.

I started going through my business travel routine—headphones out, podcast on, laptop open—looking forward to four uninterrupted hours of productivity. Then Louise started talking, so I took off my headphones and listened. That's usually not something a business traveler does. Earphones are a forcefield of protection from others—a bubble to protect from distraction. But this time was different. Listening matters. Louise was talking for a reason.

And listening is caring. She wasn't another business traveler trying to "network." But people who are scared, lonely, hurting, or lost always get my ear. You can identify those people if you look for them. Don't ignore them; find them, and do something to help them.

Louise was lonely and scared. It made me sad. I had a mission now. I learned that she hadn't flown in a long time and didn't know how to open the tray table or do much of anything a regular traveler knows. I could help her.

She had left Florida abruptly to get away from the storm coming in. And "might" have family in Denver. But she was confused and kept repeating things. She said she didn't know where she was going or who was going to help her or why she was going to Denver.

Louise talked herself into a feeling of helplessness. Loneliness. She was scared—scared of taking a trip to Denver and scared of being alone, and not sure why she was on the plane. She kept repeating all that and each time more desperately. You could see her eyes welling up.

This happens to people who are losing their memory. It's scary not to know if you have help. Some get angry, others sad. Louise was sad and blaming herself. She wasn't sure what was going on or if she would be alone far from home. She clearly had severely diminished short-term memory. She had good long-term memory but couldn't recall the day's events. She couldn't tell me much more about what was going on and couldn't remember who she was supposed to meet, or if she had wandered off from her care center. She didn't know if she had brought a phone and didn't have one with her.

I helped her with her tray table, food, and drinks. She even tried to share her food with me. We enjoyed dinner together. The air turbulence scared her, so we shared jokes to ease the fear. The woman across the aisle and I helped Louise to the bathroom and back to her seat.

I encouraged the flight attendants to make sure Louise had someone picking her up in Denver. For a while, they weren't sure as the airline scrambled to figure it all out. They were very helpful and caring.

The lady sitting near me told me she had seen someone drop Louise off at the gate. That's good news. Louise and I talked through her day and she remembered that it was her caregiver who had dropped her off, so she was supposed to be headed to Denver.

When we landed in Denver, the airline had a manager at the gate to meet Louise and make sure someone would be there to take care of her. He got her a wheelchair, too. I wrote down my cell phone number on my card and gave it to Louise, telling her to have someone call me if she needed help.

Time to go home. Mind at ease. Mission accomplished. An opportunity for kindness. What would you have done? Would you have ignored Louise or listened to her? Can you freely give to someone who needs a few hours out of your life?

We had fun. We called her a stowaway on the plane and laughed about it. I told her she was a rebel for escaping her retirement community and that her friends would be jealous of her adventures. That boosted her ego a little. We had a good time. And she had a better day. She smiled and said, "Thanks."

Thanks for your time, Louise. You also made my day.

## Leadership Takeaways

- "Stay hungry, stay humble" is a great leader's mantra.
- All the little things add up, and they matter.
- The habit of repeating the basics every day lays the foundation on which to build wins.
- If we don't try to improve every day, if we aren't always growing and learning, then we're actually getting worse because nothing stays the same. Days without personal growth are days lost.
- People make mistakes; nothing in life is perfect, either. So if you expect perfection, you're setting yourself up for a lifetime of disappointment. That's a choice.
- If you don't have accountability in your life, you won't have habits. Habits are repetitive actions that play a big role in wins.
- Pay attention to how leaders interact with others, their emotions, responses, and tactics. They offer even more insight into how you can grow and improve your own leadership skills.
- Warning signs of crumbling leadership can be subtle or gradual and usually relate to aspects of a leader's life other than business. Perhaps their relationship integrity, ethics, or honesty is slipping. Maybe the leader becomes hypocritical in what they do in their personal time compared with what they espouse in their business life. Perhaps a leader cheats on a spouse or significant other.
- When you encounter negative people, try exuding kindness. The nicer and calmer you are, the more a negative person reveals their true intentions, which eventually leads to their own demise.

- Great leaders and teachers don't provide verbatim instruction. Rather, they influence the formation of knowledge through understanding and perspective.

- How much you want to achieve something trumps knowing how to do something. That's because if you have the desire to accomplish something, you always will figure out how to get it done.

- Don't hide from your issues; you will discover that when you are vulnerable and transparent as a person and a leader, you will understand that there are many people out there who will step up to share their struggles to get your perspective and offer their love to help you with yours.

# CHAPTER 6

# From Chaos to Calm: Build Your Action Plans

*"If you're focused on fear, you're not focused on business."*

—Adam Contos

**C**haos is a sense of overwhelm that causes paralysis. Remember, overwhelm can happen when we face too many challenges simultaneously—the everyone-yelling-at-you-at-once scenario—and it can be deadly, especially for a business. That's why it's essential that leaders and their teams prepare for the inevitable chaos.

## THE BEAST IS BACK

At the root of overwhelm is fear. Action overcomes fear, so the best leaders lay out action plans or linear solutions to multidimensional challenges long before the chaos occurs.

### Not So Easy

The Beast that is chaos happens when it's least expected. But with plans for action in place, all it takes to tame the Beast when the extremes do occur are some slight adjustments to upend the chaos, drive results, and set the stage for wins. With no contingency plans, a leader must scramble to develop all new processes amid the over-whelm, and that's tough to do in a state of paralysis.

Human nature dictates that we allow ourselves to become as weak as the easy times allow. In other words, when things are easy, we defer preparing for the tough times and instead enjoy the ride. It's like lifting weights—the less weight we lift, the less muscle we build. Instead, we should continually add weights so that when faced with the heavy lifting, we are well prepared.

## Special Needs

During one economic downturn, I was working with the RE/MAX franchise sales organization to rebuild its processes for greater efficiency and effectiveness. As part of that rebuilding, we hired a script writer well-versed in the special needs associated with marketing during tough times.

When the new talking points and videos were completed, we deployed them to our sales group, expecting them to adopt the ideas and adjust their presentations accordingly. What we found instead was that people didn't like what we had done and reverted to using their old scripts. They figured nothing was wrong so why change?

They had reverted to what's easy and missed the point that special times require special needs. In general, people tend to do what's easy as long as they perceive it's working. Your processes might be working not because they are the most effective; rather, they may be working because they are minimally effective. Don't confuse the two.

Part of a leader's job is to persuade those people to do what's more difficult despite their preconceived notions to embrace the easy. By creating artificial headwinds in their business, a leader raises the bar on their staff's performance and the business' capabilities. That leader is preparing their teams for the inevitable tough times—volatility and chaos—that will surface in the future. So why not adjust for it now before you're forced to adjust amid chaos?

# VUCA

In addition to preparing ahead of time, there's a seasoned approach to deal with and overcome the chaos that simply is part of life.

VUCA, an acronym for Volatility, Uncertainty, Complexity, and Ambiguity, is a framework that spells out what happens in chaos, and it provides a formula for a leader to assess and develop action plans to drive the desired results.

## Military Beginnings

Developed by the U.S. Army War College after the Cold War, VUCA was initially designed as a framework for understanding the change from traditional battlefields to the much broader scope of the new "enemy." VUCA was a way to tame the overwhelming battle-field environment that could result from enemies hidden in unconventional places, including terrorism, propaganda, social media, and so much more. The military has since moved beyond VUCA, but it remains a beautiful leadership concept in business where leaders often lack the knowledge to move from chaos to calm.[1]

## Antithesis

To solve each of the challenges of VUCA—Volatility, Uncertainty, Complexity, and Ambiguity—and to overcome the chaos requires the antithesis of each, sometimes known as VUCA Prime. That acronym stands for Vision, Understanding, Clarity, and Agility, although I prefer the word "Action" to "Agility" since action defeats fear/overwhelm.

Action is the antithesis of fear and creates a bold feeling in the heart, which is the origin of heroism. When we recognize what creates a

---

[1] U.S. Army Culture and Heritage Center at Carlisle Barracks (Carlisle, PA), "Who First Originated the Term VUCA?" May 7, 2019 (accessed May 1, 2021), https://usawc.libanswers.com/faq/84869.

hero—people taking action during extreme difficulty—we as leaders then better understand how to be the hero during challenging times.

During the Great Recession, RE/MAX bought out its then independently owned California-Hawaii region, which was hit hard by the subprime lending and foreclosures crisis. Many in the housing industry there were overwhelmed and fearful. I was charged with operating our business in the region during the most difficult housing market since the Great Depression.

## How to Use VUCA

I understood chaos and recognized the challenges of operating in that environment. I also knew the situation needed to be contained within a framework to communicate and accomplish our mission despite the fear overwhelming so many of the businesses and people involved.

To help ensure that the rebuild of the region would be successful, I spent as much time as possible with the people to help them stay focused on the framework of working their business instead of on the fear of being overwhelmed by the business marketplace. It was like being at the beach, trying to dig a hole in the sand. You keep digging and digging, but the hole keeps filling up with sand and water. Eventually, however, when the tide goes out, you do reach a point where the hole stops refilling.

It's the same in business. You don't know when you will reach that point. But with patience and persistence eventually the problems are solved if you keep digging. In the case of the RE/MAX California-Hawaii region's recovery, it took two and a half extraordinarily taxing years. Many people gave up before it was over. Those who didn't quit built resiliency and a framework into their business that has carried them through every challenge since. It's back to being prepared ahead of time for the inevitable chaos.

## Business Perspective

Implementing the VUCA approach is the same whether someone is allocating resources for a SWAT call or for a business operation. You must identify the challenges and then take the necessary actions to reallocate the resources available. Instead of pulling back in fear, you're actually taking proactive measures to solve the challenges.

Not every effort leads to a win, but doing something—even when people don't see you doing it—is better than doing nothing. Keep in mind, too, that no matter what you do or don't do, people will criticize you. Many times it is a no-win situation. That's part of leadership. You must do what's right for your company, your people, and the situation, regardless of the critics.

# DON'T WAIT FOR CRISIS

Great leaders don't need a crisis or a wakeup call to plan and have a framework in place for the difficult times. With their internal locus of control, they take charge and guide their businesses to be ready anytime the Beast might try to rear its head. They are starting with a win.

I'm reminded of the words from a great friend and leader: *Calm seas never made a skilled sailor.*

## Confidence and Clarity

These leaders work hard to instill confidence and clarity during easy times. Their teams practice for the difficult times, too, by building the framework for success. Then when hard times arrive, all it takes is a pivot to ride out the storm and pick up the win.

For example, part of that training could include regular leadership meetings to ensure everyone understands operational expectations in good and not-so-good times. Remember, our disciplines tend to weaken when things are easy. But if we maintain the disciplines consistently, we position ourselves for the win. Too many companies fail because they fail to do so.

## Fundamentals in Place

When a leader and their company and people have strong fundamentals and a framework in place, the people who count on that leader will have confidence that together everyone can take the actions necessary to weather the challenges. Your people will seek opportunities rather than struggle to emerge from the fear associated with chaos.

Think of the training and preparation as similar to a sports team. When a great sports team plays against teams not up to its skill level and consistently wins, the great team's skills can deteriorate over time to the level of the teams they compete against. Then, if they face a tougher team, they're destroyed on the field.

As leaders each of us needs to find a way to level up our people so we're all prepared for the tougher challenges, which will happen. That's a guarantee. Also guaranteed, we grow the fastest by winning in uncertain times. So does our ability to recover from failures and to lead.

In law enforcement, we participated in "tabletop exercises," simulations to practice how to handle massive challenges like hazardous materials spills, a terrorist act, natural disaster, or weather disturbance. Businesses simulate their own challenges by assessing risks and asserting pressures on those risks to determine necessary actions and resources, and then exploring plans to handle the challenges. Businesses refer to their disaster preparation as "continuity plans" to keep the business operating in extreme circumstances.

Plan a meeting at your company with the leaders and ask "what if" to see how people react. This is forming the playbook for future challenges.

# SHARING YOUR VISIONS

Part of turning chaos to calm involves inspiring others to see the value of your vision and ideas—what's known as enrollment. It happens when others see you as the vision and choose to join you on the ride. You, the leader, create magnetism by living your vision and by being excited about the future and the change that can result from your vision.

A vision is a picture of the actions you describe that culminate in a future result. As with success, however, a vision isn't a destination. It's a stop along the way, a future measurement of where you are at some future moment, and not the end point. It's also an environment in which you place yourself.

As we describe it at RE/MAX, we create an environment where people can be as successful as they want to be. It's your vision, so what are the actions you plan to take to get there?

As a leader, it's great to have a mission, vision, values, beliefs, and so on, whether as a company or a person. But the reality is that none of it matters and your employees won't care if the leadership doesn't care about and live the mission, vision, values, and beliefs.

Sadly, employees initially always distrust leadership. Taking over as a new leader is especially difficult. Employees will begin to buy into a leader's vision and beliefs only after they repeatedly see and hear leaders use the words and phrases that demonstrate the vision, values, and beliefs of the organization. Be forewarned, though. You must be genuine, because all it takes is one slip-up to throw all that hard-won work out the window.

It's the same with a parent. You can't say it if you don't live it. Do your kids see you belittle others or abuse yourself and then tell them they shouldn't do the same thing? Leadership is being true to yourself and statements, not falsifying your life and expecting something different from those around you.

We build winning teams by demonstrating what we preach. You must live it, speak it, and uphold it. When someone doesn't do so, we have to take action. That could be private counseling or even removal from the team. Some people simply aren't a fit for your team, and your team is not a fit for them. If people can adjust to meet the standards, a leader should work with them. Those individuals who can't adjust should go.

## Leadership Takeaways

- Chaos is a sense of overwhelm that causes paralysis.

- At the root of overwhelm is fear. Action overcomes fear.

- Human nature dictates that we allow ourselves to become as weak as the easy times allow.

- Chaos involves VUCA—Volatility, Uncertainty, Complexity, and Ambiguity. To overcome the chaos requires the antithesis of each, sometimes known as VUCA Prime. That acronym stands for Vision, Understanding, Clarity, and Agility, although I prefer the word "Action" to "Agility" since action defeats fear/overwhelm.

- Great leaders don't need a crisis or a wakeup call to plan for and have a framework in place for the difficult times.

- With strong fundamentals and a framework in place, the people who count on their leader will have confidence that together everyone can take the actions necessary to weather the challenges.

- Employees begin to buy into a leader's vision and beliefs when the leader repeatedly models the behavior and uses the words and phrases that demonstrate the vision, values, and beliefs of the organization.

- Be genuine because all it takes is one slipup to throw all that hard-won work out the window.

## CHAPTER 7

## Presence and Passion: For Your People and Work

*"Want success? Build community."*

—Adam Contos

**A** business has a great product, and everyone says its leader is great. He's kind and caring and seems to have overcome his fears (the Beast). Yet no one notices the leader, the business, or its products. Its customers won't even respond to calls.

Sound familiar? This is an all-too-common scenario for many companies, especially in tough economic times when businesses struggle. If you're a leader of one of those flailing or "invisible" companies, you may feel like you're doing everything right. Still, without customers, there's no forward momentum.

Perhaps you blame the sales team for not performing or your employees for not hearing or seeing you. It may feel as if you're trying to lead in a silent room. Some business leaders lay blame on the competition or a legal or environmental issue. "I'm doing all I can" is the typical leadership refrain.

## TIME TO ACCEPT RESPONSIBILITY

As tough as this is to hear, the fault lies with leadership, and more specifically, lack of leadership. The company's leaders have disappeared, and with them trust and connection. The good news, though, is that invisible leadership is a remediable problem.

Leaders are human like employees, customers, and everyone else. They aren't exempt from pressure, stress, or overwhelm. Leaders can be strongly challenged as humans and get deeply depressed, too. Leaders, however, are supposed to know better how to deal with these human distractions.

Sometimes they do, and sometimes they don't. After all, leaders not only face their own problems but also company challenges and the life challenges of those who are in their care—their employees.

Leading is difficult, and leaders must understand that no one can lead if they are overwhelmed and unable to compartmentalize these varied issues in order to be the very best they can possibly be. To understand their own overwhelm and limitations, a leader must first be approachable and vulnerable to feedback. They must be willing to look into the mirror and see themselves from the outside and make a plan to change.

Many companies will bring in outside consultants to help leaders dig deep into their own self-imposed limitations and fears before a crisis occurs. Sometimes a conversation with a spouse or someone within an organization who can spot overwhelm is helpful, too. Similarly, coaches can help leaders by regularly looking for overwhelm or unprepared or underprepared leadership.

## LEADERSHIP COMPLICATIONS

The year 2020 magnified leadership troubles—many that had long festered. When COVID-19 lockdowns came to town, many businesses shuttered. If a business relied on face-to-face, in-person customer interaction, the challenges were immense.

Businesses quickly learned that if you can't get a customer to a cash register or point of sale, you can't sell to them. Neither can you sell a plane ticket or a concert ticket if you can't put the passenger on the plane or the fan in the venue seat. Similarly, you can't allow someone to sleep in your hotel room if they can't enter the building.

Not all businesses had to fold, though. Those like RE/MAX that creatively devised ways to keep their customers safe while serving them survived.

*If you were a customer, would you choose you?*

Other businesses rallied when restrictions were relaxed, thanks to strong connections with their customers.

## WHERE ARE THE CUSTOMERS?

For those businesses that lost their customers, keep in mind that customers don't disappear, they simply look elsewhere for similar products and services. Again, the pandemic is a great example. Many mom-and-pop and chain-store businesses closed but not because customers weren't buying; it's because now those customers looked to delivery, online ordering (and easy returns), and other means of facilitating the shopping process.

Companies like Instacart for shopping and delivery flourished. Zoom, the online meeting platform, took off—so much so in the early days of COVID and remote officing that its platform struggled to keep up with the surge. Instacart and Zoom weren't new. In fact, in 2019 Instacart was losing $25 million every month.[1] And the

---

[1] David Curry, "Instacart Revenue and Usage Statistics (2021)," *Business of Apps,* March 24, 2021 (updated May 7, 2021), https://www.businessofapps.com/data/instacart-statistics/.

first video call via the Bell Telephone Company's picturephone took place April 20, 1964, at the New York World's Fair.[2] But in the face of lockdown restrictions, consumers in 2020 turned to these apps as the way to get things done.

If a consumer could find it and purchase it online, then get it delivered physically or digitally, or pick it up curbside, then a company could transact. In the real estate industry, if someone wanted a house, a real estate agent would take a smartphone or tablet to that property and share a video with the prospective buyer. Leaders identify the challenges—the questions—and then help their people and their companies find the answers, period.

# VISIBILITY MAKES A DIFFERENCE

Once again, lessons learned from previous missions—the Great Recession—helped RE/MAX and its leaders, me included, make the right moves this time around. During the recession, the No. 1 complaint we heard as a business was, "I don't see you enough." Back then, more than a decade ago, digital wasn't as mainstream as it is today.

## The Snowball Effect

Presence creates trust, so if your people or your customers lose sight of you, they lose trust and confidence in your company and your product. Besides, you and a customer or potential client can't arrive at solutions when the two of you are arguing about whether you're present enough.

Many other businesses dealt with that issue during the recession. Those that learned the lesson rallied during the pandemic; others chose not to, and still others rallied fueled by technology.

Business leaders like to do what they see others doing, whether because of FOMO (Fear of Missing Out) or because they truly

---

[2]Daniela Hernandez, "April 24, 1964: Picturephone Dials Up First Transcontinental Video Call," *Wired,* April 28, 2012.

see someone doing what they know they should be doing. Due to the ease of distribution created by social media platforms, during the pandemic businesses watched each other online and mimicked what they saw.

Success on social media isn't hard to duplicate. The key is consistency to net results. The businesses that got ahead of the lockdown by jumping instantly on marketing platforms to stay in touch with their customer base did well; the same was true with leaders. Top of mind definitely proved effective in 2020.

# VIRTUAL CHALLENGES

The pandemic brought another set of challenges for businesses. As virtual reality became business reality, this different approach in this altered environment raised its own set of questions:

- How do consumers find companies?
- How can companies be "seen" by these consumers?
- How does a company maintain that presence in front of the consumer?

The answers, again, all revolved around presence. Until recently, few consumers ever saw the CEO of a business. Think about it; do you know the CEO of your grocery? Only a select few people really cared about what a business or its leader stood for, either. But that changed as social consciousness became more widespread in 2020. Of course, again, that concept wasn't new, but COVID changed people's minds. Faces behind the business began to matter. Three words took precedence—trust, safety, and inclusion.

Many leaders struggled to approach those topics or initially had difficulty finding the right "talk tracks" for fear they would be misrepresented or offend communities. Others literally hid, mostly for fear of causing problems for their employees or companies. Some, though, stood tall and shared.

## BUILDING TRUST THROUGH SOCIAL MEDIA

These company leaders became more visible as they sought to build a new trust and convince the public it was OK and safe to do business with them. People suddenly wanted to know that you care before knowing that you can help them. Consumers didn't necessarily want to know all the safety protocols a business had established, but they did expect businesses to reach out and let them know that the business was open and able to help.

The transition was tough, especially for those leaders more accustomed to issuing insensitive written text with liability issues top of mind. Rather, this new consumer expected and continues to expect leaders to interpersonally connect clearly with meaning and kindness via video broadcasts on social media and other broadcast media.

Those leaders who lost out—flopped or disappeared—did so because of the Beast in the form of FOPO: Fear of Other People's Opinions. Their personal Beast whispered in their ears that someone might disapprove if they do this new thing and embrace this new approach to doing business. "It's not how a CEO acts" is one statement I heard. My saying: No Mo FOPO.

It's the same reason so many people are afraid of public speaking. Sure, the first time you jump up on stage or turn on a live broadcast from your iPhone so anyone around the world can see, you stumble. It's likely scary, too. As I mentioned earlier, I still feel the fear before I address a large crowd. That's just part of the process. What you do with the fear is what matters.

And it gets easier with practice. Those are the missions that teach us and become part of our playbook for life.

## HUMANITY AND VULNERABILITY MATTER

Consumers today want a consistently transparent, present leader, who is willing to show vulnerability and humanity (more on that later). This became more apparent as leaders were unable to get in front of employees and customers with health regulations. As a result, leaders needed to get better fast.

Most CEOs hate shooting unscripted video, but consumers want it. That's a big if not rude awakening for business leaders more accustomed to operating quietly behind the scenes. But believe it, today's consumers and customers actually appreciate your fear of speaking on video and your stepping up and talking about an uneasy or difficult situation. Rather than revealing a leader as too vulnerable, it shows they care.

Most leaders and decision-makers do care. They take very seriously their responsibility for the lives and livelihoods of others. They don't want to botch what they say on camera, but people need to know that they are human and they care.

For today's business leaders, it's OK to hop in front of a camera and thank customers for their support; a leader is allowed to admit that they care, or that they don't have an answer, but the team is working hard to find a way to make a difference. This kind of presence creates trust and builds crucial relationships with the consumers.

The transparency of a human presence—where it's OK to make mistakes—adds to the genuine, caring approach of someone's leadership. People want true commentary and feelings. That's real leadership, leaders who display vulnerable presence.

---

*Say something nice in the elevator.*

---

RE/MAX believes in being actively engaged in creating a presence with our customers, employees, and partners. A strong presence is even more important in times of uncertainty and crisis. When circumstances demanded it, we redesigned our playbook for a deeper, more engaged representation of our leadership. We connected more than ever before simply by being more present.

As CEO, I've appeared in videos—often multiple times in one day during the lockdown. We would be on video broadcast across four social media platforms—Facebook, LinkedIn, YouTube, and

Instagram—discussing leadership principles, kindness, and how to be better at all you do.

Actually, for any leader interested in building client and consumer relationships, regular presence-building videos are a simple exercise. All that's needed is a computer with a webcam or a smartphone and a little know-how. Check out YouTube for an array of quick tutorials. What matters is that people can see your eyes, your smile, and your face so they know you care. Lighting and audio also matter so that you appear clear and are easily understood.

RE/MAX also instituted a weekly live video broadcast Mind, Body, Business. Each week we chose one word as the theme and examined how practicing that attribute could make each of us a better person and help those around us. For example, a theme word might be Caring, Consistency, Kindness, Excellence, and so on. The broadcasts also included a downloadable document with more information.

## YOU CAN DO IT!

Before you as leader think this is well-beyond your expertise or time frame, consider that the videos I mentioned above were created in my basement! I was cameraman, sound technician, lighting director, and technical producer. I tested the internet feed, focused the camera, and set up all parts. And trust me, I'm no tech wizard. I learned it all from scratch during the pandemic. I always was a video fan, but this forced me personally to learn how to do it all myself.

All that social media presence worked, too. I earned the confidence of those with whom I connected. These people—many of them real estate agents—watched me do it and realized they could do it, too. All that was required—the slight tailwind mentioned at the beginning of this book—was validation that the timing was right to engage with customers to rekindle the caring that had been established pre-COVID shutdown. Remember the 80 percent rule—be willing to accept less than perfect—and realize that some video is better than none at all. Don't freeze or take flight; take action.

Business coach Jon Cheplak offers this simple formula for a video: Don't sell, just care. He frequently says, "My crappy video is better than your nonexistent video." And he's right. Some video presence, even of mediocre quality, is better than none. If you call a client to follow up via a phone call or personal video, for example, ask how they are doing, and be sincere. The connection is about replicating in-person intimacy. As a leader, it's essential to genuinely care when talking with customers because if you don't, they know.

## BUILDING CONNECTIONS

As digital presence gains in popularity and demand and as businesses increase their digital presence, these businesses also become more imbedded in their communities. Customer relationships grow and develop. Our agents have made huge strides in community and customer connection by shooting localized videos. Someone may do an interview or review of the local pizza place or ice cream parlor. Or they may interview someone from the local chamber of commerce or even take a series of videos featuring the best parks to enjoy with your kids. No matter the intention, these videos create localized content that search engines reward with good optimization online, they create more presence for a business, and ultimately they create more customers.

Social media matters. Marketing in many cases has moved beyond paid placements to encompass personal and home videos describing how much people care about each other. The iPhone and other smartphones have become among the most powerful communications tools on the planet as small businesses create hours of video designed to let people know they're still in business. This is how leaders start with a win by building connection and creating trust. This is how leaders demonstrate being present.

## OUT OF LINE

"Out of sight, out of touch" is for outdated leadership that is no leadership at all. That kind of myopia is why companies fall out of line in life and business. We see throughout life and in these pages that the ability to connect with people is the solution.

Many leaders have lost that ability to connect and have disappeared from view. Most embrace excuses and blame their lack of presence and connection on economics or world crises or both. Or they lie low, worried about the implications of saying the wrong thing. Maybe their marketing teams also advised them, "No, now isn't the time for you to be visible." Or the worst excuse of all: They simply haven't adapted to change and have failed to focus on connecting.

Whatever the reasons, the consequences are the same—out of sight is out of touch. If your customers can't see you, the reality today is that you don't exist for them. This goes for your employees, too, as well as any businesses you interact with like suppliers, vendors, or partners. When you fall off the radar, you're relegated to the back of the line in business.

## TOP OF MIND

The bottom line: Top of mind is first in line. And, yes, I'm still talking about presence and passion. A goal for a leader or for a business that interacts with society is to be first in line when someone thinks about your service, product, or industry.

If a company's name—its brand—isn't synonymous with its service or product, that company may as well not exist. A brand, personal or business, carries a promise of value and how it is to be delivered. This is known as a brand promise. What's your brand promise?

When we think of a hamburger, usually McDonald's comes to mind. Facial tissues are Kleenex; aluminum foil used to be Reynolds

Wrap. For a time, the iPad was the tablet. Google is the verb. Xerox used to be a verb until it wasn't, and the competition overcame it.

Whether the product or service is the best or not, it's the brand that stands out. People know what they get when they think of the brand.

# BRANDING AND PRESENCE

This is why personal branding works so well. The power of branding is especially evident today with today's social media influencers. Your personal brand is you: your association with others; the value, the empathy, the transparency you deliver; and your brand promise, which is the words that people use to describe you.

As a leader, you represent two brand promises—the brand promise of your company and the brand promise of yourself. Both present a promise of how a consumer will be treated, and the effort involved to meet their needs.

A brand matters because your brand is how you are perceived by others—your presence. It's an expression of the emotion and experience you deliver. It's your intimacy or lack thereof.

Social media influencers have focused on building personal brands for more than a decade. Check out YouTube, Facebook, Instagram, and Twitter—they're packed with influencers who have established their brands and co-brands, and who now transact business. Branding gets other people to notice, be interested, trust, and become invested in a product or service.

Branding helps branding. That's why brands associate with other brands, which is known as co-branding. Companies often team up with influencers to build on their company brand. They also spend lots of money to do so rather than spend the money on more traditional paid advertising. Your leadership position doesn't matter—you could be a teacher, real estate agent, salesperson, or whoever. But as you begin to brand yourself and find another brand with which to co-brand, your voice is magnified. Then, with presence and passion, you will connect.

# BRANDS DISAPPEAR

Brands don't evaporate overnight. They fade away if they're no longer fresh and usable. The biggest problem of many people is that they become complacent. If the memory people associate with a brand is decades old, the brand fades, unless it is successfully reinvented, and that can be tough. A brand can't rest on its laurels or afford to cut back too drastically on marketing, advertising, and presence.

**Fresh.** There's a reason brands like RE/MAX continue to stay top of mind. We reinvest in its marketing every day. Apple does the same and stays fresh and relevant. Apple has people wanting "what's next" even though there is nothing wrong with what they have right now. You don't know what you need until they tell you what you need and you say, "I didn't know I needed that," but somehow now you do.

This is what you should think about when considering your brand. How do you adapt and continue to stay relevant without losing your place in the consumer's mind? A company can't go from selling cars to selling hamburgers and stay relevant within that genre. You sell cars or something related to cars and stay relevant. The adaptation of gas to electric cars is a good example of a brand staying relevant.

**The generation dilemma.** Does your brand consistently market to one generation? If so, is your company ready with new and different marketing strategies for when that generation fades from the marketplace? Millennials want to be marketed to completely differently from Baby Boomers now in their 60s, and 70s. A brand, after all, doesn't want to necessarily be known as "my grandparent's brand." Some brands have tried to evolve with generations to attract mainstream buyers. "This is not your father's Oldsmobile," for example. How did that work out for the General Motors' Oldsmobile vehicle brand? Who even remembers the Oldsmobile? Its last vehicle rolled off the assembly line in 2004.[3]

---

[3] Editors at History.com, "The End of the Road for Oldsmobile," A&E Television Networks, November 13, 2009, updated April 27, 2020 (accessed May 25, 2021), https://www.history.com/this-day-in-history/the-end-of-the-road-for-oldsmobile.

Brands that are fresh-faced stand up to change because their leaders know that brands must change to stay top of mind. Remember, top of mind is first in line. People look for brands to evolve and to appeal to new generations with new needs and desires.

## THE VALUE OF PASSION

Without passion for your work, your people, or your industry, you're neither doing your best nor living up to your full potential. If you're a leader, you're also letting down all those people who look to you for guidance and strength.

I love my company; I love the people in the company, and I love the industry. The people energize me to work together with them and to better the organization because I know it helps them.

The job of leader comes with tremendous responsibility. If you lead a company, pressure comes from all the stakeholders and must be balanced with economic and market positions, social pressures, and the unknowns. Those unknowns include whatever disaster may occur and impact the business.

As we've all seen in the past few years, disasters can assume many shapes and sizes, from natural disasters to terrorism, to public safety concerns about tainted products and the like, and so much more. In the face of such disasters a leader must step out and stand out with their words, deeds, empathy, and compassion.

As an example, when there's a major natural disaster or tragic event, government leaders always offer words of condolence and financial or medical assistance to victims or victims' families if necessary. Why? Because that's one more thing that's expected of leaders.

When India was hard hit with massive numbers of COVID-19 cases and oxygen shortages during the pandemic, countries and individual companies stepped up to provide oxygen canisters, medical assistance, and more, to help save lives.

## WEIGHT OF RESPONSIBILITIES

As CEO of a public company, I regularly pitch our company and its value to potential investors, answer difficult questions on quarterly earnings calls, and take the stage to speak with large groups of analysts, investors, and industry people at conferences. As the leader, I do all this while balancing the responsibilities of taking care of our customers and employees, being visible and present, and fulfilling our brand promise.

We may have 600 employees in our holding company, but that means 600 families for whom I'm responsible. It's the same for our network of 8,700 offices in 110 countries and more than 140,000 agents. I feel responsible for all of them and their families, and I enjoy the focus that brings to my decisions.

What truly matters, though, is that I have the opportunity to serve them every day. I'm humbled by that opportunity, which allows me to express my passion for my people and my job. I also experience a great sense of gratification with the wins. Their wins are my wins. They did 1.78 million transaction sides in 2020—during the pandemic. (A transaction side in real estate is half of the transaction—either bringing the seller to the transaction with the product or the buyer to purchase it.)

Think of how many families they helped—how many people they helped find a place of happiness. That is what keeps me going.

Whether you lead a big company, a small one, or simply a team, many of the responsibilities are the same. Others count on you; they look to you for direction and guidance as well as decision-making. They need to know you are visible and that you care.

## MORE MUSINGS OF A CHILD

As a child, I always admired superheroes. I watched them in the movies and on television and wondered what made these normal people superheroes. People listened to them; they answered hard questions and always seemed to have the right answer. And they had confidence.

I admired other leaders in movies who behaved the same way. It didn't take a company crisis or special situation for these great leaders to be present. They just stood up with confidence and communicated; they created followers and solved problems. The concept infatuated me.

These leaders remained calm and collected and talked their way through and out of situations. I saw this in my parents, my uncle, and other great people around me. These people didn't lose their bearing or become upset easily. They were kind and generous and treated others with dignity, caring, and respect. These are the role model leaders.

## OPPORTUNITIES TO LEARN AND GROW

As a leader, I appreciate the challenges and opportunities, the fears and setbacks, and the passion for people who want to improve. I also understand that sometimes we get tired and frustrated. Most likely you feel this way as well. Appreciate it. We're human, and business and leadership are about human beings.

I feel the weight of this responsibility. It's called accountability, and it's fuel for leaders. Unfortunately, too often people mistakenly associate accountability with condemnation. That viewpoint is ingrained in us from an early age. We are raised by our parents to be held accountable, which means being condemned for something we did or didn't do. But that's not the best approach to understanding accountability. In the truest sense, after all, accountability is noticing without judgment—that is witnessing actions objectively and not judging with emotions.

The leadership suggestions and concepts in these pages are not about condemnation or polarity of viewpoints for whatever someone is or isn't, or has or has not done. Rather, they are about providing each of us with a sense of accountability or an internal pressure to exert on ourselves to be better. It's not a question of either/or. Each of us is unique, as are our missions. Therefore, the routes each of us take to our wins may be different, but the framework remains the same.

## YOUR TURN

Now it's your turn to think about your leadership, your approach, and your brand promise as a person, a leader, a parent, a friend, an influencer. It's time to audit yourself—who you are as a leader and how you present yourself to others.

The results of that audit can illustrate the benefits you offer others as well as the hurdles and challenges you face to build yourself and your business.

## THINK ABOUT YOUR BRAND

Ask yourself some of the following questions and be honest in your answers:

- What is your brand promise?
- What is your brand statement?
- When people see you on video, what do they learn about you?
- In a video or other presentation, how do you come across to others—as caring, stoic, confident, wishy-washy, unsure, sad, happy, confused, angry, intelligent, lost?
- How would you like to be perceived by others?

Here are a few additional ideas to consider when auditing your brand:

- What illuminates you?
- Why do others want to be around you?

- Why do others seek you out?
- If someone drew you as a cartoon character, what would the character be doing?
- What words describe your "look"? Are you proud of it? What would you change?
- What is your alter ego?
- What is your super-power?
- If you were in a movie, would your character be a hero, a villain, or an extra?
- If you spoke to a high school or college class, what would the topic be?
- What do your last 10 social media posts say about you? Do you sound happy, sad, angry, polarizing, afraid, motivated, dedicated, lost, or something else?

## PATTERNS AND CONUNDRUMS

After you've thought about these questions and answers, do you notice a pattern? Are your thoughts aligned, or are they scattered all over the place? The picture you describe, your brand, indicates not only how people see you and your business, but also the outcomes they expect when they associate with you or your business. You should see some parallel directional trends that are in sync with each other. You should see consistency in how your company and how you present yourselves. They should align.

Remember, to start with a win and continue those wins requires consistency, kindness, and caring as well as the ability to promote trust, safety, and inclusion. This is your presence, your ability to be an effective leader. This is the emotion and experience you deliver, your intimacy. Those you work with and encounter in your business and life will trust something about you. They know what it is; do you?

What people trust about you is your reputation—what they say about you in your absence. If that reputation isn't consistent or clear, consider taking whatever time necessary to align your thoughts with your actions. Then you won't present a confusing conundrum to others, including your customers and your friends.

# BE SELECTIVE AND HONEST

Remember the old saying, "Stop trying to be everything to everyone"? It's absolutely true in your personal life and in business that you can't be all things to all people. We can't please everyone, so it's best to be wisely selective in the promises we make. People prefer that you say no up front rather than promise them something and then disappoint them at the back end by not following through with the commitment or product.

A great old fable I heard years ago illustrates my point. The fable is long, but the lesson is well worth learning:

A long time ago, an old man and his son needed to get to market to sell their ass. The journey was a long one, so they set off early one morning. They were walking the donkey down the path and came across a farmer working his field. The farmer asked the old man, "Hey, old man, why are you both walking? That boy isn't going to be able to work for you if he gets too tired so early in the day."

So the old man looked at the boy and said, "Let's conserve your energy; get up on the ass." They continued on toward the market with the old man walking and the boy riding the donkey. A little while later, they encountered another man walking along the path who asked the old man, "Why are you walking, old man. You have a long way to go. Why don't you ride the donkey and save your energy also?"

The old man agreed and climbed onto the donkey with the boy, and they continued their journey to the market. As the day wore on and they came closer to the market, they encountered a group of women. One of them said to the old man, "Hey, old man, you're wearing out your ass. Look how tired it is. If you are going to sell that ass at market, you better not wear it out."

The old man and boy got off the ass and decided they better carry it the rest of the way to market—just over the bridge—so it had energy and could fetch a better price.

They started carrying the ass over the rickety old bridge separating them from the market. As they crossed the bridge over the stream, the ass looked down. Scared by the fast-flowing water, it started to struggle. The old man and the boy carrying the ass lost their grip, and the ass fell off the bridge into the stream and was swept away to its death.

The old man and the boy, tired from their struggle, managed to get to the other side of the bridge and collapsed. The boy asked the old man, "What happened?"

The old man looked at the boy and said, "Son, let this be a lesson to you. If you try to please everyone, you will never get your ass to market."

# USE YOUR JUDGMENT

This is a common problem in all types of businesses. Leaders often listen to too many people when trying to accomplish something, and they never get to market. Everyone has an opinion about how you should proceed, but few offer to help.

Do what *you* think is right to get to market. Don't overpromise. We should focus instead on what *can* be accomplished and do it well. Otherwise, others lose confidence in the business and its leaders. Perhaps even worse, you lose confidence in yourself and end up struggling to find your identity.

Keep in mind that confidence is the No. 1 leadership trait that attracts others. So align your brand, display your confidence, be present, build relationships, and go for the win.

## Leadership Takeaways

- Presence creates trust, whether with your employees, customers, or community.

- Get on social media. Your presence as a business leader is required.

- Consumers today want a consistently transparent, present leader, who is willing to show vulnerability and humanity.

- Top of mind is first in line. A goal for a leader or for a business that interacts with society is to be first in line when someone thinks about your service, product, or industry.

- Without passion for your work, your people, or your industry, you're neither doing your best nor living up to your full potential. If you're a leader, you're also letting down all those people who look to you for guidance and strength.

- As a leader, appreciate the challenges and the opportunities.

- Accountability is fuel for leaders; it is not condemnation, for which it is commonly mistaken.

- As a leader, you represent two brand promises—the brand promise of your company and the brand promise of yourself. Both present a promise of how a consumer will be treated, and the effort involved to meet their needs.

- Think about your leadership, your approach, and your brand promise as a person, a leader, a parent, a friend, an influencer. This is who you are as a leader and how you present yourself to others.

- The results of that audit can illustrate the benefits you offer others as well as the hurdles and challenges you face to build yourself and your business.

- To start with a win and continue those wins requires consistency, kindness, and caring as well as the ability to promote trust, safety, and inclusion. This is your presence, your ability to be an effective leader.

- Do what you think is right to get your product or service to market. Leaders often listen to too many people when trying to accomplish something, and they never get to market.

# CHAPTER 8

# Lose the Ego

*"Don't be a know-it-all. Be a give-it-all."*

—Adam Contos

**D**on't let wins lead to failures. That happens more often than you think because the biggest challenge facing a leader isn't persuading others to follow or deconstructing challenges and developing solutions. A leader's biggest nemesis is an ego spun out of control.

Sometimes a leader whose company finds success forgets that it's the company and its people who deserve the praise. The leader, as their ego takes control, begins to use the word "I" instead of "we" or the "team" and animosity builds among employees and internal leaders. They begin to leave or underperform and eventually the leader's demise will follow.

As leaders we must recognize that a team inherently will praise and support its leader for taking the risk of failures. But also remember that the leader should be the first to take any failures off the shoulders of their team and the first to allow the team to bask in their wins.

## THE BEAST IS BACK

Simplified, an ego is insecurity, an emotional response (the Beast is back!) that is triggered to protect someone from their own vulnerabilities. When a person allows their ego to take control, figuratively they put up their fists to prove a willingness to fight for personal gratification.

It's a false sense of self-actualization (achieving your full potential) as opposed to being vulnerable and giving self-actualization (sincerity).

## AN EXCUSE

Someone usually manifests a big ego to conceal their ignorance or inability to perform a particular task. Those with big egos typically offer little help to others and rarely care about others or their projects because they feel such trivialities are beneath them.

Traditional workplaces with their top-down organization promote big egos. The people who rise to power try to position themselves as better than others instead of lifting others up. The latter approach is the mark of a true leader, but the big ego is more concerned with besting others than leading them. Yes, a structure of accountability and decision-making is necessary, but titles should be earned and not given. When someone leverages a job title rather than earns it, it's the Beast—their ego—in control.

## PLAYING AS A TEAM

None of us can completely deny our ego because when combined with knowledge, giving, and position it designates authority, decision-making, and responsibility. But we need far less ego when everyone on a team works to lift up its leader because that person helps the team grow intrinsically in the organization. It's the old saying, "There's no 'I' in team."

The egotistical "leader" places blame; the humble leader tries to deliver help and hope. As some of the stories I've recounted demonstrate, while in law enforcement, I tried to deliver that help and hope.

I learned long ago when I joined the Marines that I wasn't working for myself. I was working for the organization of which I was a part. The Marines are an example of selflessness because Marines will die for each other. Would your co-workers die for you? Would you die for them?

Most people would say no because their work is just a job and a means to a paycheck. But even if you aren't willing to die for the person in the cubicle next to yours, the principles of giving and self-lessness still apply. Either way, you must set aside your ego. If you can't honestly say that you are trying your best to lift up that other person in their career and life, you're protecting your ego. If you refuse to help your co-worker because that person isn't pulling their weight, then do something about it.

## HUMILITY MATTERS

One of the egos you confront looks back at you in the mirror every morning. An ego simply is part of who we are as humans. It's natural. But we need to be intentional in how we use our egos. We can direct our egos by deploying humility and accepting unconditional responsibility through extreme emotional intelligence.

Some of the ways to tame our ego involve our choice of words and approach—for example asking others, "How can I help?" or "How can I make this better for you?" as opposed to being accusatory and asking, "Why in the world did you do that?" The egotistical tend to be conclusion jumpers and narcissists. They believe that if they can attack someone else, it elevates them in their own mind and empowers their ego.

When a leader is humble and willing to ask others—and not just their peers—for advice, help, and constructive criticism, that leader also builds strong relationships with many of those individuals. The result is allies who can and do magnify that leader's message at a peer level. That's extremely powerful.

## HANDLE WITH CAUTION

Unfortunately, we can find egomaniacs at all levels of business. These are the people who quickly jump on the innocent mistakes of others in order to elevate themselves. At the same time, these people are very quick to conceal their own mistakes by wrongly blaming others. They hide behind blame, judgment, and condemnation.

The reality is that people make mistakes, especially when they are trying their best to accomplish something. Leaders know how to accept an honest mistake. The egotistical expect perfection without appreciation for trial and error.

The biggest egomaniac I ever observed didn't get what they wanted in life, so this person threw a fit, upended an organization, and nearly took the business down with them. As soon as you determine that someone in your organization is an egomaniac, you need to help them exit your team as soon as possible. Otherwise, the specter of havoc will be a constant concern hanging over your organization.

To hone your leadership skills, try this simple exercise. Think of five to ten of the most obvious egomaniacs you have encountered in business. Write down their names or some other identifier so you'll recognize each one. Then ask yourself how that person could have reduced the size of their ego, and what that simple action would have meant that person's success.

You will be surprised at how successful someone can become if they decide to keep the ego in check. Tame the Beast.

## HOW DO YOU ACCEPT CRITICISM?

Here's another way to study egos. Consider this simple question courtesy of coach turned Silicon Valley guru Bill Campbell: "Are you coachable?" Campbell has coached Silicon Valley legends including Apple's co-founder and former CEO Steve Jobs, Google co-founder Larry Page, Eric Schmidt also of Google fame, and Amazon's Jeff Bezos.

*"You can't tell someone the truth when they believe they already know it."*

—Kelly Contos

## LISTENING SKILLS

Think about Campbell's question for a moment. Are you receptive to other people's ideas and suggestions for personal improvement? If the answer is no, then you're essentially admitting that your ego prevents you from being vulnerable and accepting necessary change. This is narcissism, one of the killers of leadership.

Merriam-Webster defines a narcissist as an extremely self-centered person who has an exaggerated sense of self-importance. In other words, someone who requires admiration, lacks empathy, and basically cares only about themself, period.

Beware of narcissists in business as well as in your personal life. These people will inhibit your growth and make you unhappy if you don't sever ties with them.

## SEIZE THE OPPORTUNITY

The formula for leadership and success requires that we learn to control our emotions and move beyond fear into a framework for creating opportunities.

When the Beast—in this case fear-guided ego—rears its head, view it as a fork in the road. You have a decision to make: Do I become emotional and allow my ego to assume control? Or do I become opportunistic and seek the framework for solutions. In every situation, you have the choice.

## THE POWER OF WORDS

Choose your words carefully in situations that might trigger your ego to surface or when someone else's ego takes over.

The use of the word "concern" (e.g., "That concerns me.") is an emotional response that pushes ugly egos to the surface. It is an ego tool to block others. However, approaching the same situation and using the words "How do we" (solve this) or "How do we" (achieve that) lays out a constructive framework for solutions. When a person defaults to the blame scenario, they trigger emotional responses and defensiveness in others.

Another word to avoid is "overwhelmed." Again, the word triggers an emotional response. Rather than be overwhelmed, opt to be constructive and think about the underlying causes of a situation. Overwhelm simply means that you're thinking of too many things at once. The warning sign that overwhelm is seeping into the psyche is when people keep repeating the word "busy." Each of us has the choice to be busy or productive. Busy is defensive. Productive is offensive.

## BREAK DOWN THE CHALLENGE

So instead of allowing your ego to take control and blaming others for a challenge or problem, make a list of everything that you're worried about (overwhelmed by) at the moment. Cross off the list things those things that really don't matter, then one by one assess and act on each remaining item on the list. When a challenge is solved, cross it off the list.

This is an easy way to break down problems into manageable pieces and deal with them as challenges instead of burdens. Other words that trigger emotions and require this kind of deconstruction include "frustrated" and "afraid." It's easy to use these words in conversation, but if we think about our words before we speak, we set ourselves up to be closer to a win than to something less.

## KNOW THE "NO"

Another word that carries hidden meaning well beyond its literal definition is "no." The reality is that when someone says no to a proposal, project, suggestion, sale, or whatever, it's not necessarily a finality. Depending on the circumstances, "no" generally isn't an end-of-the-world answer.

It's important to analyze the context of the rejection. Why did someone say no to you? Was it because that person didn't have the time to spare? Or maybe the resources were lacking? Maybe they said no because they didn't have the funding or they were afraid, or they didn't consider the situation a priority. In these scenarios, "no" can be mitigated. That's why it's so important to listen to the words and the context of the words. You must know the "no."

## MAYBE "YES"

Saying no can carry a myriad of meanings. It could mean that the person is really saying yes to something else because when someone says no to one thing, they are saying yes to another. Inversely, when you say yes to something, that sets the scene for saying yes to other things. A well-known sales technique calls for beginning a pitch with questions that lead the potential customer to say yes to a few simple things. That leads to a string of yeses and it becomes harder to say no. Watch out for that.

I know this sounds a bit confusing, but "no" is also a "spot or position protector" in life. We have only so much time in a day and only so many things that can be accomplished in life, so "no" could be a gatekeeper to allow an extra spot in case something else—some better or more important opportunity—comes up. That's why it's so important to understand the context and the shades of "no."

Remember earlier I discussed my daughter Maggie's ability to accomplish so much in her freshman year of college? That's because she mastered the "no" in her decision-making. Her high emotional maturity enabled her to make choices based on their impact on her obligations. And "no" contributed to her ability to accomplish what she wanted.

## "NO" LEADS

Many leaders in big business, myself included, say no much more often than yes. I respect that. If you have a product or service, it's important to understand that it is your product or service that can turn the initial no into a yes. The product or service provides the hope and overcomes the challenge. Without hope or solutions, it's harder to achieve a yes.

If you can't understand that and are unable to break through, then you and your product or service are not considered a top priority. And if it's not a "Hell, yes!" then that's a no in my world. Respect this when someone else tells you no. Just remember that they might be thinking along the same lines you are.

In other words, it's your product or service that must elicit the yes response. If it doesn't, step back and figure out why. Look at the challenge, assess the options, and then make the changes necessary to get to yes.

## CROSSING THE CHASM

Some friends have a startup business that sells a SaaS (software as a service) product. In the beginning early adopters snatched up the product, and my friends got super excited; they were on their way to big success, or so they assumed. Then once my friends began their marketing campaign and reaching out to sell their product to strangers, they began to get "no" from potential customers. Of course, my friends were disappointed and frustrated. So we sat down and talked.

Most business begins and transactions happen based on relationships. Someone must have a relationship of trust with you to do business with you. Without that prior relationship, potential customers are skeptical. Hopefully, though, the early adopters allow others to see the value of your product or service to generate additional business.

# FALSE STARTS

Nonetheless, after that early flurry comes the natural chasm or gap in the development of a business. That happens to almost every business and is especially common among sales positions. After those first sales, everything slows down substantially for an unknown length of time. It can get lonely trying to find a yes at this point no matter how hard you search.

I look at the early adopters' phase really as a period of false starts or false results. The sales to this point aren't indicative of how the mainstream market will accept you or your product or service. Those people who have purchased your product or service to this point might have done so based on the fact that they know you or have done business with you in the past, or they are the rare breed of extreme risk-takers. Beyond that point, it's up to you to get people excited about going from no to yes regarding your product or service. Most people at this point are still in the "huh?" stages on your product or service. They just don't know enough to make a decision.

It's the same in life. When you move to a new place, for example, the early adopters welcome you. But then comes the chasm—the lonely place—until others recognize your value. Sometimes it's easier to bridge the chasm when we realize that there is another side and that we eventually will get there.

Those businesses and people who don't understand what's happening and who don't have the patience to work their way through this gap in sales are the businesses and people who fail.

Those "no" responses that tank the business occur because there's no reason for a "yes." Also, the business owner expects other people to know as much as they do about their product or service and how great it is. After all, the early adopters did. This is known as the curse of knowledge that plagues business owners.

Don't ever assume people know your product or service as well as you do. That's why the very best in sales can tell someone about their company, product, or service as if that potential customer is a five-year-old. If you can't do that, you will likely struggle to gain customers.

## TRUST BUILDING

To get potential customers from "huh?" or "no" to "yes" requires a trust-building phase. A new business or product must give value unconditionally and repeatedly to earn a buyer's trust and attention. That's true more now than ever before because of the noise and negativity that bombard us every day.

When a business owner can cross the chasm and persuade people to accept the value of a product or service, then the real growth in a company occurs. That's the norm, whether the business involves a police officer trying to prevent or encourage certain behavior or a consumer or business-to-business customer whose life can be made easier or more comfortable because of your product or service.

Once my friends understood that what was happening in their SaaS business was part of the natural framework for a new business and necessary in the relationship-building process, and not to take it personally, they knew where they had to take action. They implemented more processes to help get potential customers to the trust phase through a deeper understanding of these potential clients' challenges and how their product solves those problems.

My friends didn't quit, and their business began to truly take off.

## INGRAINED

As my friends learned, "no" can be a very damaging word if we don't dissect its true meaning and understand its context. When you were growing up, "no" meant you were condemned by your parents or teachers or friends. "No" was an attack on your ego, your fun, freedom, and future. That's how we're raised.

Unfortunately, no one has come up with a different word for kids being told they can't do something or for a business being condemned by too many "no thanks." The feeling is the same in both situations if you don't understand that "no" simply means you and your team haven't done a good enough job of enrolling others—potential customers—in your dream product or service.

## SELF-LIMITING BELIEFS

How often have you been told no in your business and thought to yourself, "I can't do this"? If you're like most people, the answer to that question is probably many times. More importantly, how did you react after hearing no? Did you quit, or did you keep trying? Many people in that situation quit, especially if they and their business are stuck in the chasm between early adopters and mainstream acceptance. It can feel overwhelming.

Whether related to business or your personal life, our perceived shortcomings and self-limiting beliefs too often restrict our accomplishments. That mind trick relates to the Pike Syndrome. Nearly 150 years ago, German scientist Karl Mobius placed a large predator pike in a fish tank and then added its favorite food, minnows. The pike ate the minnows. Then Mobius added more minnows to the tank, but this time they were separated from the pike by a glass barrier. The pike, oblivious to the separation, charged at the minnows, only to ram the glass. After several unsuccessful attempts to get to the minnows, the pike gave up. Even after Mobius removed the barrier, the pike refused to pursue the minnows. Sounds like the chasm in business!

Remember, success may be just on the other side of your final failure. Believe it, and don't quit. Don't self-impose unnecessary restrictions and know that on the other side of failure, success likely is waiting.

## OVERCOMING "NO"

As I mentioned, most startups don't get beyond the "no" and fail as a result. What those business owners miss is that life and business aren't about finding the "yes." They're about finding the excitement that fuels others to say yes.

Life and business both are built on countless micro "yeses"—wins along the way. And both life and business involve giving in order to get, which leads to relationships. And relationships lead to purchases by your early adopters. Now is the tough part, though—getting the "yes" from those people who have "no" in mind. If you can earn a "yes" from them, eventually that can add up to more and bigger "yes" responses and relationships and transactions.

Businesses function on relationships built on a foundation of trust. You do something for someone else, so they trust you. Then they want to do business with you.

It's as simple as that when it comes to sales and when sales agents feel like they're not getting anywhere.

Another way to help you get past the chasm stall is to measure and monitor the results of your efforts to deliver value. Understand that it requires consistency and endurance to establish trust. It's not a one-time action; it's a long-term commitment to create and share before you see any results.

Getting beyond the chasm also is about being a good person and giving to help others. Know, too, that you will give away your best information for free, but that's a deposit into your life account that will pay interest later.

The solution I offered my friends was to give away information, expertise, advice, and presence, then call potential customers and find out how they're doing. Learn their challenges, and send them solutions. Think of the initial "no" as "Make me like you so much that I want to do business with you" instead. That's how you start with a win even in the face of "no."

Those same steps apply today, and they start with doing things for other people free of charge to help them and to show others that you and your business can provide value. People want solutions to their challenges. If you can help, you build relationships that can last and yield potential customers as well as positive recommendations to others.

## Leadership Takeaways

- The biggest challenge a leader faces is an ego spun out of control.

- An ego is an insecurity, an emotional response triggered to protect someone's own vulnerabilities—perhaps ignorance or inability to perform a task.

- The egotistical leader places blame; the humble leader tries to deliver help and hope.

- Egomaniacs are the people who quickly jump on the innocent mistakes of others to elevate themselves. At the same time, these people are very quick to conceal their own mistakes, hiding behind blame, judgment, and condemnation.

- The reality is that people make mistakes, especially when they are trying their best to accomplish something. Leaders know how to accept an honest mistake. The egotistical expect perfection without appreciation for trial and error.

- Ego also is human nature. We can direct our egos by deploying humility and accepting unconditional responsibility through extreme emotional intelligence.

- Most business begins and transactions happen based on relationships of trust.

- When starting a business, the early sales generally create a false start based on past relationships. After the early flurry, though, comes the natural chasm or gap until you can sell the mainstream buyer on the value of your product or service.

- In business you will give away your best information for free, but that's a deposit into your life account that will pay interest later.

- "No" is a word that carries hidden meaning well beyond its literal definition. When someone says no to a proposal, project, suggestion, sale, or whatever, it's not necessarily a finality. Depending on the circumstances, "no" could mean "possibly" or "down the road" or "the money isn't available right now" and so much more. Know the "no."

- To get potential customers from "no" to "yes" requires a trust-building phase. A new business or product must give value unconditionally and repeatedly to earn a buyer's trust.

# CHAPTER 9

# The Trifecta: Mentor/Coach/Mastermind

*"Be strong enough to listen, wise enough to ask, and kind enough to help."*

—Adam Contos

**E**veryone needs someone to talk to whether as a sounding board for ideas, a source for advice, an experienced leader for guidance, or simply a willing ear to listen. Mentors, coaches, and masterminds provide all that and more. Find all three and you hit the trifecta of wins. Sometimes some of those people find you.

## THE MENTOR

One evening while still a cop, I was working an off-duty job at a golf course under construction. There had been theft and vandalism at the work site, so my job was to ensure no one entered the premises after dark. I was sitting in my car in the middle of the night when a flashy new Chevrolet Suburban pulled up. Out climbed an energetic man, about 50 years old, smiling broadly and looking very excited. He rushed over to introduce himself as Dave, the owner of the private course.

Dave then invited me to check the property with him. I hopped into the passenger seat of the Suburban, and we took off. Keep in mind that it was dark and this was a mountain course with very steep terrain, so it was tough to see much of anything in our surroundings. That didn't slow Dave at all. He shifted the Suburban into four-wheel low and we were off across the 240 acres of wilderness amid various construction obstacles and piles of dirt. Dave was one of the most fun people I had ever met and seemed unfazed by the challenging terrain he was attacking with his new SUV. It was a blast!

We made it to the farthest, most secluded area of the course unscathed. Then while driving up very steep terrain we ran over several large sections of plastic covering the newly paved concrete cart path. The plastic quickly wrapped around the SUV's drive shaft, and we came to a halt with a large ball of plastic stuck under the vehicle.

Dave and I looked at each other—we had never met before that night—and at about the same time said, "Got a knife? Let's fix it!" We ended up under the vehicle on a hillside in the middle of the night with flashlights and knives in hand talking about everything imaginable as we worked to free the SUV. That was my introduction to my mentor.

## Mentor Extraordinaire

That night, Dave and I built a friendship and the beginnings of a mentorship that's still going strong nearly three decades later. Dave has taught me how to learn from other leaders, what to look for in them, and how to grow my own leadership. He has counseled me about life and business. He still freely shares his experience and his perspective, because as with other mentors, he has an intrinsic desire to make society better by helping create leaders who take action. He's a giver and one of the most generous philanthropists and kindest people I've ever met.

We discuss life and business, from process and strategy to relationships and people. We make major decisions together and support each other. Sometimes he will debrief me on choices I make or business decisions our company pursues. He asks questions, we unpack our thoughts, and we evaluate risks and opportunities. We intensely argue our points with each other, often disagreeing, but remaining agreeable and respectful of each other's ideas and concepts. He watches my on-stage speaking engagements and offers in-depth critiques to help me grow.

The most important part of Dave's input is that I act on his suggestions. When he suggests a book or an article to read, the next time we see each other, I've read the article or book and am prepared to discuss it. When he suggests research on a business or topic, I do that too.

Dave does his part as a mentor, and I do mine as a mentee.

## Valuable Insights

Mentors understand human nature and leadership, and they have experience or perspective in your business space. Often that experience includes overcoming extraordinary business and personal challenges to find success and developing others into key organizational leaders. They likely have been pushed hard to grow and have discovered ways to deconstruct the results of their labors in order to share them with others.

As with Dave and me, a mentor has a close personal relationship with their students. A mentor facilitates growth; they do not give it. A mentor indicates areas where there are doors to open. You must find the doors yourself, have the guts to open them, and walk through them to become better every day.

Some of the best advice Dave has ever offered deals with human nature. He wasn't responding to a question or situation, but instead talking about why he does certain things. Dave deeply cares about others who care, who have the best intentions, and who have the desire to learn and do better. He has low tolerance for people who are lazy and self-serving. And he can read others incredibly well, articulating his thoughts with extreme detail.

## Finding Your Right Sounding Board

When looking for a mentor, find someone who wants to be available to you. However, you must be available, too. Keep in mind that *you* cater to the mentor, not the other way around. Leaders should meet with a mentor at least monthly but it can be more or less frequent depending on schedules and needs.

---
*Be a role model for someone; it makes a difference.*

---

Though mentors are not paid in cash for their services, you pay them with your attention. They pay you, too, by sharing time and wisdom.

If you seek leadership, you'll find it. But if you don't actively look, you may miss those leaders who could help you most. I always searched for leadership and success principles in law enforcement mentors, and that helped me see leaders even when other people took them for granted.

One day while still in law enforcement, I was standing at the window of the sheriff's office building talking to a long-time commander and looking at the parking lot full of patrol cars. He offered a piece of advice that sticks with me still today: "Just remember this: In order for an organization to get better consistently, it's imperative for leaders like me to step aside and allow leaders like you to take over."

He meant it, too, and put in for his retirement not long after our conversation.

His profound statement is one that all leaders must consider—how do we help the next generation of leaders become so good that we are proud to step aside and watch them take over. Great leaders and mentors help each of us realize the counterintuitive. Many leaders with egos or fear of letting go won't even consider helping others learn so they can take over.

Great leaders, though, know when to step aside. They mentor the next generation. Those are the leaders who can help you become a better problem-solver and a more impactful leader if you learn their philosophies, observe their trials and tribulations, and emulate what works. It's all about interactions, emotions, response, and tactics. When we see someone achieve something positive, often we're inspired to achieve on our own, too. A person can be inspired by not so positive achievement as well, so be careful whom you choose to emulate.

# THE COACH

Unlike a mentor, a coach—business and otherwise—gets paid for their services. In exchange, a coach helps you to unlock your potential and understand your shortcomings. Leaders should meet with a coach at least every other week and sometimes weekly. Coaches are high-touch, high-performance drivers for leaders.

## Holistic Advice

As with leadership, coaching is holistic. How does a business coach know if you're having problems in your personal life? Because your business performance will be severely lacking.

When you struggle in one aspect of your life, you struggle in others because failing at one thing often undermines your drive to succeed elsewhere.

Our self-limiting beliefs can permeate all of our habits and efforts. The frustrations far outweighed the successes when I worked in California during the Great Recession. When losses compound, lives tend to spin out of control. It was survival mode—lack of sleep, poor eating and exercise habits, and degraded relationships.

To prevent that, we must recognize and plan for successes. We all will face challenges in life, so we *must* build in successes. Otherwise, self-limiting beliefs take over and we expect less from ourselves. Like the pike that gave up on the minnows, we can starve by allowing some failures to keep us from trying to succeed. We end up moving from an effort mindset to an existence mindset. Instead, the harder life becomes, the more intentional our successes must be built into our schedules.

## The Details

Some coaches also are psychologists. One of six paid coaches in my life was a psychologist who helped me to define my strengths through a series of psychological tests and processes. This coach and her team of great coaches also worked with my leadership team to identify their strengths, thus bringing great continuity to our leadership development.

Coaches ask questions, give advice, and help you create moments of self-discovery. They tweak little things in your life and business that make a difference. Ultimately, however, they do not tell you what to do but rather point you in a direction. It's up to you to decide what you're capable of and then to take action.

## Lonely Road

Not long ago I saw a longtime friend and successful CEO of a franchise company at a convention. I asked him how he was doing, and he asked me if I had a coach. I looked at him and could see he was trying not to cry.

I asked, "Are you OK?" He just looked at me. I said, "It's lonely at the top," and he said, "Yes." I asked if he thought his stress—burnout—was holding back his company, and he said, "I know it is."

Luckily my friend knew that a positive attitude is a learned behavior, and that with coaching, he could successfully relearn positivity. And he recognized the importance of reaching out to others for help. It was a simple yet life-changing conversation for him.

I've burned out, and I've struggled like everyone else. I understand the internal struggle leaders face, and I make the conscious decision to take positive steps to help ease the stress. Your attitudes and actions are your decisions. Think holistically and act holistically, too.

# MASTERMIND

Masterminds are groups of top performers (master minds) who collectively influence change. I think of masterminds as a group of people who gather, in person or virtually, to help each other improve individually and collectively by asking questions to create thoughts, aha moments, and reflections.

## The Details

Some masterminds are free; others are paid—anywhere from a few hundred to tens of thousands of dollars annually. Some high-level masterminds can cost much more. I prefer paid masterminds because when people pay for knowledge, they pay more attention in pursuit of a positive return on investment. In other words, when you attend a mastermind, you expect to leave and implement enough change in your life or business that you see a substantial return on the investment required to attend. Masterminds truly work.

Masterminds usually require specialized facilitation skills to host and uncover hidden value in you, your situation, and your company. Be aware of this and understand how to put the knowledge you gain into play. But start attending them and participate. You'll be surprised at how much you can learn and grow as a result.

Of note: Free masterminds are more like feel-good moments and ego strokes than change events. Similarly, discounted events generally are used to sell a product or service.

## The Right One

Finding the right mastermind is critical. This isn't about learning a new sales technique or attending a mega-seminar with motivational speakers selling products. Rather, the purpose of a mastermind is to stimulate transformation and cause realization/clarity to effect difficult decisions. Small changes occur, certainly, but many times a breakthrough moment occurs as well. If you are on video for a mastermind, there's less impact. Online masterminds simply don't offer the same accountability and vulnerability of in-person sessions. That's tough in these videocentric times.

Most people who attend masterminds also end up with at least one accountability partner, someone from the group who will support, critique, and celebrate you, and who will help you push for results, and vice versa. It's important to make these relationships and keep them going as trusted confidants. In fact, any time you find a great success partner, take advantage of it whether the connection is through video or in person.

I am part of a group that meets virtually for accountability but strives for one or two in-person meetings annually, often in a retreat setting. Usually we spend a few days together bonding and talking, along with scheduled face-to-face meetings as a group. We allow ourselves to be vulnerable regarding our businesses and our self-improvement. These sessions are life-changing and are a key reason that I have been able to achieve what I have in my life.

Discretion and absolute trust are essential to a successful mastermind.

## Traits of a Mastermind

Just showing up doesn't cut it for a mastermind. It takes preparation, determination, and grit, too. A few helpful hints if you decide to join a mastermind:

- Lose the ego at the door.
- Preparation: Don't just show up; prepare ahead of time. Bring information to share, challenges as well as successes to discuss, aha moments, life hacks, and any other information or perspectives that could be valuable in an honest, open, high-level discussion.
- Perspective: Recognize that you will leave with a perspective different from when you arrived.
- Respect: Understand that you must be vulnerable and respect others who are as well. Everyone's feedback is valuable; listen to it and respect their energy. Be 100 percent focused; no multi-tasking. That means turn off the cell phone.

- Confidentiality. Violating this tenet typically means immediate removal from the group. No one is comfortable discussing their biggest challenges and opportunities around someone who can't keep a secret.

- Give: You are here to give as much as you possibly can, but not to take over. Masterminds have a designated facilitator who generally is paid out of proceeds for any fees paid to attend. (Of note: That's not always the case, however. I am in a mastermind that has no designated facilitator. The group takes turns "hosting" the event. Finding that kind of a groups is very difficult. Our self-hosted group has been together for nearly a decade. Each of us has experience facilitating high-level masterminds, and coming from other masterminds, we've all shared time in a paid mastermind environment.)

- Grow: Be willing to be pushed to grow like never before. If you can't handle the discomfort of a hard conversation with your most trusted peers, masterminds aren't for you. In these sessions, you may disclose a challenge or process in order to get pointed feedback. Often that feedback includes challenging perspectives and ideas that may help validate a decision you face. I have seen people learn that they needed to fire high-level employees, relinquish control to others who are outperforming their leadership, change long-standing business relationships that have run their course but are still in effect out of loyalty, and much more. A mastermind must be a place of vulnerable growth, and if you aren't willing to use it as that, don't join one.

# FINDING THE RIGHT MENTOR, COACH, OR MASTERMIND

There are several ways to find the right mentor, coach, or mastermind, depending on your business interests. You can contact various industry, business, and professional organizations to see if any have lists of related, reputable masterminds seeking new members or participants, qualified business and life coaches, and even potential mentors. Networking with business and professional contacts is another option as are organizations like SCORE and related U.S. Small Business Administration groups and incubator organizations.

If there is an expert, specialist, or educator you follow or admire, Google their name and "mastermind" to see if they offer or participate in a mastermind. Or you can Google "mastermind." But be very careful if choosing the latter approach. All types of for-profit sales groups and organizations claim to be mastermind specialists. The same caution applies to coaches and mentors, too.

If your business relies on or has relied on investors like venture capitalists, those people or organizations often may be able to suggest a coach, mentor, or mastermind or help you form a mastermind of your own. Colleges and universities may have lists of qualified individuals interested in helping, too.

Also, talk to friends, business colleagues, and even your indirect competitors. Any or all of those people may offer valuable insights into whom to approach or where to go for great information and direction.

No matter how you identify a potential coach, mentor, or mastermind, check out the person or the group thoroughly before you plunk down any cash.

Once you've identified a potential coach, mentor, or mastermind group, ask yourself whether you're comfortable speaking with the person or the group. What do you need from or what do you have to offer to the person or group? There aren't any right or wrong answers to those questions, and don't expect everyone to be a perfect fit. Take your time and understand that finding the right person or group likely will take trial and error. Just recognize that the effort upfront will be worth it.

## FAMILY TIES

Any discussion of role models and advice-givers must include family. For many of us, our first guidance comes from our parents or loved ones. For others, the lessons learned may not be positive, but they are learned nonetheless and shape the beginnings of who we are and how we do business.

My father taught me the only thing you can lose is your integrity; don't, or you'll be poor for life. In other words, tell the truth and respect yourself. Those are timeless, wise words in business and in life. Doing the right thing and telling the truth, no matter how difficult, always matters.

So does a solid work ethic and the willingness always to do a quality job and do it on time and with courtesy, saying "please" and "thank you." As simple and mundane as this sounds, too many people in business have forgotten some of the essentials and courtesy. These tenets play a role in developing long-term relationships that matter, especially in business.

Giving back to your community matters, too, as does treating others with dignity, respect, and compassion. The little things do matter!

## THE VALUE OF A THIRD PARTY

People often think that they can develop their leadership skills on their own. But none of us can be expected to notice all of our faults or even identify all the opportunities. That's why it's important to find the right coach and mentor and participate in mastermind groups. Without this vulnerability and constant multifaceted approach to personal growth, we're unlikely to regularly raise the bar for ourselves.

Getting hired as a leader, manager, CEO or whatever is only the beginning. To maximize your performance is still up to you. The feedback from third parties like mentors, masterminds, and coaches is designed to effectively manage your growth and the growth of those around you.

Too often we overlook the value these third parties bring to our growth and development and fail to avail ourselves of the opportunities. Some of the reasons are that these third-party advisors are costly, time-consuming, embarrassing, uncomfortable, and leave us vulnerable.

Leaders don't like to step down and allow themselves to be vulnerable. It's imposter syndrome—fear of being found out as a fraud—mixed with fear of the opinions of others. Both, of course, are irrational, yet they're real fears that reawaken the Beast in all of us.

The reality is that working with coaches, mentors, and masterminds is an excellent way to tackle the Beast—address your fears, attack them head on, and come out learning serious lessons—for the big win.

# GRATITUDE

Whether each of us agrees with the feedback from these coaches, mentors, and masterminds, their input is valuable knowledge to be unpacked and assessed. How do you accept it? That's simple; say, "Thank you." That's right, even if you're insulted and upset, say thanks.

Try it and watch how those giving the feedback react. In whatever situation and whatever the feedback, saying thanks prompts people to engage with you. It's the same with your customers and potential clients. If someone is unhappy or happy with you, saying, "Thank you" makes a difference. You're really saying, "I respect that." As I said earlier, simple words like these opens doors, and people appreciate them no matter the situation.

That extends well beyond coaches, mentors, and masterminds. When we make even small gestures of gratitude to others, we engage with them and learn about them, their experiences positive and not so, and make their lives a little better. By learning if a customer is having a bad day, for example, you can possibly improve it and possibly even earn a lifelong customer simply by caring about their feelings. Again, it's the little things, the details, that make a difference.

Most people shut out feedback that doesn't feel good. Don't; feedback is an opportunity to learn and grow.

## Leadership Takeaways

- Mentors understand human nature, leadership, and have experience in your business space. Often that experience includes overcoming extraordinary business and personal challenges.

- To find a mentor, look for someone who wants to be available to you. However, you must be available, too. Keep in mind that *you* cater to the mentor, not the other way around.

- Actively look for leaders. These leaders can help you become a better problem-solver and a more impactful leader if you learn their philosophies, observe their trials and tribulations, and emulate what works. It's all about interactions, emotions, response, and tactics.

- Coaches ask questions, give advice, and help you create moments of self-discovery. They do not, however, tell you what to do, but rather point you in a direction. It's up to you to decide what you're capable of and then to take action.

- Just showing up doesn't cut it for a mastermind. It takes preparation, determination, and grit. Be sure to ditch your ego at the door, too.

- If there is an expert, specialist, or educator you follow or admire, Google their name and "mastermind" to see if they have a mastermind or participate in one.

- Be careful when choosing a coach, mentor, or mastermind. Do your homework, look for references and referrals, and make sure the person or group isn't simply trying to sell you something.

- If your business relies on or has relied on investors like venture capitalists, those people or organizations often may be able to suggest a coach, mentor, or mastermind or help you form a mastermind of your own. Colleges and universities may have lists of qualified individuals interested in helping, too.

- Too often we overlook the tremendous value third parties can bring to our growth and development and fail to avail ourselves of those opportunities.

- Whether you agree with the feedback from coaches, mentors, and masterminds, their input is valuable knowledge.

- Express gratitude by saying thanks.

# CHAPTER 10

# Celebrate the Wins

*"Listen to the birds—your team—singing."*

—Adam Contos

**T**ake the time to appreciate your wins, no matter how big or small. A win is a personal creation, a piece of art that's the result of hard work and dedication to a goal. Like an artist, we should take the time to enjoy our masterpieces.

This isn't gloating over a victory. A leader of one or 100,000 doesn't flash their ego as leverage. Celebrating a win is taking a moment to appreciate the final product—the win—and to thank those who took the journey with you.

## POWER OF HOPE

Celebrating achievements also is about reinforcing hope—the hope to win again and again and again. Hope, after all, is the energy that fuels wins.

## BRAIN RECALL

Imagine that you just completed your first marathon, something you thought unattainable. After you catch your breath, hydrate, and rest, you take the time to pause and let your feat sink in. You revel in the accomplishment and the feeling of satisfaction that goes with it.

The moment isn't so much about celebration as it is allowing your brain to recall your success and make the mission—the race—a permanent part of your playbook of life. After all, there's another marathon in a few months that you just may want to enter, too.

A business win is the same thing; it's a challenge that takes smarts, planning, practice, stamina, and action to overcome—a different kind of strategy, planning, stamina, and practice, but a plan and execution nonetheless, and no less of a feat.

## THE RIGHT WAY

At RE/MAX's annual convention recently, we took the time to talk about all the hard work and extra effort everyone had put in to pull out our win. As I mentioned earlier, despite the COVID-19 lockdown, RE/MAX had one of its best years ever in 2020.

So we paused to celebrate our accomplishments; we had earned the celebration. Every year, thousands of our agents and brokers gather to celebrate. I have the privilege of handing out awards, talking with these winners, hugging them, and sharing meals with them. We take photos together, too, because it's a time for us to truly appreciate each other. When we're done celebrating, we return to our home cities and celebrate again, this time with our own teams.

All the hoopla goes back to Dale Carnegie's two things we can't give ourselves—personal attention and appreciation. This is our opportunity to give ourselves both.

> *"Two things we can't give ourselves are personal attention and appreciation."*[1]
>
> —Dale Carnegie

## LISTEN TO THE "SINGING"

Happy people make noise. They talk, laugh, celebrate, collaborate, and work together for great things. Whether at home or at work, challenges become discussions that create solutions and wins. Those wins are celebrated, and the cycle continues.

Visit an amazing company and you will hear the noise and feel the culture of winning that comes from the top—the leadership. But what happens when the positive leadership and the music—the celebration of wins—stop? Stress and overwhelm take over; it's heads down, do the job. Interactions stop. Leaders don't hold meetings or notice outstanding efforts, and people stop winning.

Not long ago I sat down with leaders of a large organization to discuss the importance of recognition, leadership, and opportunities. We talked about how wins begin with leadership. That can be a tough task for a leader during chaotic and overwhelming times in the heat of business battle or personal problems. Making fixes in a fragile company easily swayed by a leader's bad day or a market shift is not easy, nor is it a destination. But it must be done.

Restoring a winning culture isn't an overnight process, either, because when a leader falters and the culture stumbles, that leader must earn back their employees' trust. It's the bank account of life discussed earlier—we need to deposit many more positives into the account to overcome a single negative. The leader sets the tone and

---

[1]Dale Carnegie, *How to Win Friends and Influence People* (New York: Simon & Schuster, 2010).

pace for a happy, motivated, productive team. But it's a team effort—once the team is convinced of its leader's authenticity and caring.

## CELEBRATING LEADERSHIP

Celebrating the wins demonstrates positive leadership. Teams connect with leaders, and leadership overcomes management.

That matters because leaders model, influence, and create value, while managers direct with power, numbers, and the bottom line in mind.[2] Managers suppress leaders; they oversee them, too.

Managing in the absence of real leadership isn't good enough because when management takes over, it limits a leader's ability to lead. Managers also prevent leaders from seeing the results of their efforts—the necessary gratification. Wins aren't celebrated; leaders leave and take employees with them because people follow great leaders. Or, worse, leaders may be stripped of their leadership capability by an organizational chart that places experienced managers in charge. That can happen because of a change at the top levels of a company, a demanding regimen from shareholders, a board of directors hyper-focused on managing instead of leading, or even because of industry or regulatory fears/influence.

Managers manage results, while leaders influence greater results by motivating people to dig deeper out of drive and produce better results. For example, a company has a senior vice president who is an excellent leader and positively influences the enthusiasm and actions among company employees. But the vice president under them is a structured manager who relies heavily on numbers and relentlessly drives results. That manager's voice is the loudest and, as a result, robs the business of its leadership. Workers are held accountable instead of being motivated by leadership.

To prevent such erosions of leadership, a company needs to celebrate its leaders, not stifle them. True leaders live for the chase and

---

[2] Navar Vineet, "Three Differences Between Managers and Leaders," *Harvard Business Review,* August 2, 2013, https://hbr.org/2013/08/tests-of-a-leadership-transition.

the feeling of accomplishment, as compared with managers, who want to follow the numbers and the process and thus drag people down to that level.

## When We Don't Celebrate . . .

During the leadership meeting mentioned above, I opened the conversation by describing the leaders' wins. Their faces lit up with pride when I talked about them. It's back to the importance of self-actualization and the power of appreciation.

## Overlooked Wins

Clearly these leaders, like so many others in the top tiers of leadership, hadn't received the recognition they deserved, especially in the presence of their peers. Again, leaders are human. We should celebrate everyone's wins. By starting with the celebration, I built a foundation of trust. These leaders knew up front that I cared enough to talk about their accomplishments, and as a result, they cared enough to open up to me.

Wins are important for a business or a team, regardless of the nature of the win, its size, or how it's celebrated. Just make sure it's celebrated. Leaders generally are so focused on the challenges they face organizationally that they often forget to stop and celebrate their own wins. If something isn't going right, leaders often blame themselves because they feel an obligation to take care of the team. But we all need to give ourselves grace. We can't always expect to win and then move on to the next challenge again and again.

Stop to celebrate the accomplishments; otherwise, we can fall into the trap of always expecting other people to win. Then a win becomes a monotonous task and is no longer a win—it's a burden.

Even celebrating consistent operations should be a cause for celebration. Many organizations with inherent safety issues, for example, like manufacturing or industrial operations, take the opportunity to celebrate the lack of accidents. That's a big win in their business, as it should be. Businesses like restaurants might celebrate how quickly they turn tables, or the number of meals returned to the kitchen, or the waste ratio of food.

In the above examples, we're looking at smaller, incremental accomplishments, but those are just as important as major wins and should be celebrated too.

## Fostering Animosity

As these leaders and I talked more about their company, we found that some wins weren't reported or were suppressed to protect departments and silos. Animosity grew as a result. That can happen when a leader in a vertical organization like theirs—as opposed to a collaborative, team environment—celebrates their group wins, while their peers in other parts of the organization don't.

That creates imbalance among employees across the larger organization because they see the celebration and don't understand why their similar efforts aren't recognized.

## Analyzing the Challenge

Looking more closely at the situation, we recognized that the company was top shelf, exceeding its peers, and scoring lots of wins thanks to its people. They can take pride in their governance and operational excellence.

Yet even the best can eat themselves from within. And that's what was happening with this company. Organizations and companies don't fall apart overnight; it is usually a slow, painful, and progressive death. This self-destruction begins with the syndrome of expectation versus appreciation. When the frequency of wins drops, so do the celebrations. Employees and leaders begin to turn inward; they lose enthusiasm and begin to harbor fear. They focus on protecting their jobs as opposed to taking calculated risks to improve.

## Danger of Territorialism

I've seen this situation happen before. It's called managing a career, not leading it. Such a leader gets their team to a point where they meet and manage those expectations while also protecting themselves from scrutiny. They "get by" without stretching forward—that is, without adding any risk.

The situation creates a fragile environment in which employees become restless and then frustrated. The wins no longer matter; people go into survival mode—doing what is expected and nothing more. The risk of winning overcomes the risk of the company falling apart.

Sure, there still are some amazing players in the company, but they're suppressed by those with territorial and protectionist attitudes. Egos get in the way of growth. Siloed management takes over. People turn their attentions inward to manage the silo instead of leading. And the slow death spiral begins.

(Remember, a real leader contributes to the organization as a whole and encourages everyone to do better. It also often requires giving—whether it's manpower, resources, budgets, or something else—on the part of some in the organization so another can succeed.)

This spiral within the silo spreads throughout the organization and begins to take down other silos, which have formed due to the competitive and protective nature of the silo managers. They argue about who owns a success and project their failures onto others. This overt attempt to protect failures by building walls of bragging, meeting metrics, and more allows the failures to go unfixed and encourages managers to focus only on how best to describe their metrics.

## Stop the Downward Spiral

How do we prevent an organization from eating itself from within? By celebrating the wins across the organization. That means celebrating across siloes, too, which inherently demonstrates vulnerability and encourages others to try to outperform you. Celebrate that, too.

When we lift each other up and build community within an organization, we help to break down walls, and we all get better together.
Vulnerability and celebration of the vulnerability build stronger organizations, too.

It's not easy for a leadership team to get started on this path, and
it can only happen when there is trust. Trust and its essential vulnerability lead to conversation and transparency among various departments, which in turn leads to efforts to help across departments
because there is no ego barrier.

# KEY PEOPLE INDICATORS
# AND RETURN ON WINS

We slap fancy business acronyms on metrics that help rate financial
success or its lack. Two important metrics are key performance indicators (KPI) and return on investment (ROI). Both are lists of what
we witness; they are results.

Key performance indicators could include sales numbers (and the
litany of marketing and prospecting numbers), revenues, expenses,
profits, days sales outstanding, customer lifetime value, and more,
depending on the business and the industry. If we don't look at KPIs,
dashboard them, and understand them, we can miss opportunities
and fail to notice gaps that can cause the slow spiral of death for
a business.

### KPI 2.0

The same goes for what I refer to as KPI 2.0, Key People Indicators.
Life KPIs benchmark happiness, health, relationships, spirituality,
wealth, and stress. As leaders, if we don't pay attention to KPI 2.0,
our people will collapse.

When we look at the results of our leadership, we must ask ourselves these questions:

- Is there evidence of our leadership? That is, how do our people perform?

- Are they making noise?
- Is productivity celebrated and is the sentiment positive and growth-oriented?
- Do people help each other willingly and without ego barriers?
- Do they trust the organization, leadership, and their co-workers to do what's best for each other and everyone?
- Do they work through challenges and difficulties and understand that failures happen and must be taken with a learning mindset?

It's important to quantify your answers to these questions and pay attention to the results. Key People Indicators tell the real tale of your business.

## ROW

Similarly, for the traditional return on investment, ROI 2.0 becomes ROW, Return on Wins. As leaders, we need to see our people celebrating wins. Is that happening? If it is, the celebrations add tailwinds to boost the culture, values, and sentiment of the organization. You step back and proudly watch as people acknowledge what they have been through, the recognition and appreciation they receive, and their well-earned right to celebrate.

## Your North Star

Think about KPI 2.0 and ROW. Do you and your company's Key People Indicators and Return on Wins reflect what you as a leader are trying to accomplish? Can you even measure KPI or ROW, or are you and your company still in survival mode?

When you use these two ideas as a North Star to begin your quest for wins, you'll know you're headed in the right direction.

The amazing part of RE/MAX is that the company focuses heavily on these cultural tailwinds. Our organization is so proud of the wins of our network of super achievers that we get together to celebrate them frequently. I am honored to send out congratulatory videos, which are shared in their offices and around social media. As discussed earlier, our team hosts an amazing awards ceremony, complete with Hollywood-style glamour and excitement.

Our network of winners proudly walks across the stage in front of thousands to receive their trophies for excellence in helping so many people realize their dream of home ownership. When is the last time you or your organization had an appreciation event for employees and customers? Try celebrating your relationships and reap the dividends.

## THE RIGHT WAY TO CELEBRATE

When it comes to determining the best way to celebrate those wins, go big, go small, or pick a reward somewhere in between. The important thing is to notice the wins and honor the work required to get the win.

It's particularly fun to give big prizes to employees for big accomplishments. At RE/MAX, for example, we celebrate an employee's long tenure—30 years—by giving the superstar and their spouse a free trip to Hawaii.

We celebrate small, too, with bonuses or fun events. A well-deserved and certainly appreciated small celebration can be as simple as giving someone an extra day off. We call those MORE days. The MORE comes from our company's value statement mentioned earlier:

- Deliver to the Max.
- Be customer Obsessed.
- Do the Right thing.
- Together Everybody wins.

Whatever you, your team, or your business do to honor achievement, it's about celebrating to give hope, providing encouragement to do one more—whatever form one more takes, and gracious giving back to create a win, win, win for the person, the company, and for you.

## Leadership Takeaways

- Celebrating achievements also is about reinforcing hope—the hope to win again and again and again. Hope, after all, is the energy that fuels wins.

- Happy people make noise. They talk, laugh, celebrate, collaborate, and work together for great things. Challenges become discussions that create solutions and wins. Those wins are celebrated, and the cycle continues.

- Celebrating the wins demonstrates positive leadership. Teams connect with leaders, who empower and inspire others. That's compared with management, which rules by the bottom line and numbers.

- Restoring a winning culture isn't an overnight process. A leader must rebuild trust, and that takes time and patience.

- Wins are important in a business or team, regardless of the nature of the win, its size, or the style of celebration. Wins by leaders are important to celebrate, too.

- Beware of territorialism in your organization. It can tank the wins and eat away at an organization from within.

- Think of key performance indicators (KPI) as KPI 2.0, Key People Indicators. Your people tell the real tale of your business's success or not.

- The traditional return on investment (ROI) becomes ROW, Return on Wins. When you the celebrate the wins, you add tailwinds to boost the culture, values, and sentiment of the organization.

- Stop to celebrate the accomplishments. Otherwise, you can fall into the trap of expecting the win. Then the win becomes a monotonous task—a burden.

# Good Reads

*It's Your Ship: Management Techniques from the Best Damn Ship in the Navy*, by D. Michael Abrashoff

*Trillion Dollar Coach: The Leadership Playbook of Silicon Valley's Bill Campbell*, by Eric Schmidt, Jonathan Rosenberg, and Alan Eagle

*The Success Principles. How to Get from Where You Are to Where You Want to Be*, by Jack Canfield

*How to Win Friends and Influence People*, by Dale Carnegie

*Influence: The Psychology of Persuasion*, by Robert Chialdini

*Atomic Habits: An Easy & Proven Way to Build Good Habits & Break Bad Ones*, by James Clear

*Good to Great*, by Jim Collins

*Great by Choice*, by Jim Collins

*The Power of Habit: Why We Do What We Do in Life and Business*, by Charles Duhigg

*The Compound Effect: Jumpstart Your Income, Your Life, Your Success*, by Darren Hardy

*Living Your Best Year Ever: A Proven System for Achieving Big Goals*, by Darren Hardy

*Think and Grow Rich*, by Napoleon Hill

*The Fifth Discipline: The Art & Practice of the Learning Organization*, by Peter Senge

*Discipline Equals Freedom*, by Jocko Willink

# Acknowledgments

**S**ome amazing people helped me create the life behind this book, and the book itself. These are people who helped me when I had doubts about myself and who gave me a nudge and who believed in me—or challenged me to be better. You made me look up when I was looking down. You let me see a different way, and you helped me step through challenges I might have shied away from. You made a difference in someone's life and in this world. Your presence on this planet helped shape me into who I am and helped me put that creation into these pages. I sincerely thank all of you for that great gift. And please know we aren't done yet!

The love of my life, my wife and best friend, Kelly: You have loved and supported me, adventured with me, and grown with me. You have pushed me to get better, helped me see my faults and attack them with dignity and kindness, and believed in me in my crazy ideas—including the idea of writing this book. You are my 5 a.m. workout partner, scuba buddy, and life coach. Each chapter in our lives together seems to get more adventurous and exciting, which is the greatest gift you could possibly give someone—the experience of spending your life with someone you love. You are an amazing mom to our kids and dogs, a fair and compassionate human being, seeker of knowledge and improvement, and a loving partner in life.

My parents, Frank and Margie: You raised me well. You taught me values, honesty, integrity, and kindness. You gave me an example of how to be great parents and set the bar high for me to try and achieve. I love that we are so very close and appreciate all that you bring to me and my family's lives.

To my kids, Ashleigh, Jack, and Maggie: Each of you brings different gifts to my life and to this book. It's an honor to be on the ride of life with all of you. From being a single parent to Ashleigh to adopting Jack and Maggie, I love you all so much and in such a special way. You have supported me in my efforts to be the best I can be and continue to push me beyond my imagination.

My brother and sister, Christian and Katie: Thank you for being lifelong friends and believing in me. You inspire me with your caring and giving, and you set a great example of kindness.

To my Uncle Kevin: You were my hero growing up and pushed me to seek the bravery I saw in you—from the Marines to your calm confidence (with a healthy dose of crazy humor).

Dave: My mentor, best friend, brother from a different mother, and one of the best leaders anyone could ever follow, you have helped me sculpt this life with your light nudges and heavy shoves. We have laughed, cried, failed, and succeeded together. You are an amazing person and such a great influence on my life and successes.

Gail: You have given me a viewpoint on life, leadership, and kindness. You deliver humor in the greatest ways and smiles even in the most challenging storms with your amazing ways of seeing reality. Your stoic presence and kindness have greatly influenced my life and learnings. Thank you!

Darren: A great friend to me and mentor to many leaders globally, your wisdom and perspective are second to none and your framework for success has been incredibly influential to my growth. You were a leader to me but have become a great friend and confidant in the process. Thank you for your transparency and vulnerability. You and Georgia are a gift to Kelly and me and we love you both dearly. Be the exception!

To my friends and colleagues in masterminds, my coaches, and mentors, and a special shout-out to my friends in the Dozen: I cannot begin to describe the impact that my relationship with each of you has had. You can see the difference all of you have made. The results speak for themselves.

Producer Mark: You have enlightened me and helped me grow with your creativity and artistic perspective. Your kindness and smile are "so good" to see when we work together. Your help in getting *Start With a Win* off the ground was a blessing. I am grateful for our friendship.

Susan: You have brought so much to my dream of having my thoughts in a book. Your amazing questions and experience have given me the opportunity to produce this incredible work. I sincerely thank you.

Zach and the John Wiley publishing team: You called me one day and said, "Let's do this"—something that I have always wanted to accomplish. You set the bar and pushed me to get over it. Thank you for believing in me and my story.

To my friends with whom I have been honored to serve our country and our communities, to help the hurting and charge into danger with: The courage I saw in you during our most trying— and sometimes most rewarding—times has given me strength and humility. You are too numerous to list, but I honor you and your desire to help and give. Thank you!

To all of my amazing friends, colleagues, partners and customers in the RE/MAX holdings family—agents, broker owners, office staff, employees, MLOs, directors, and team: You have given me the platform to lead and made me earn it every day. I thank you for this opportunity to serve all of you and do my best to help you achieve MORE. You are the greatest network of entrepreneurs on the planet. Keep giving, helping, and growing, and never settle for anything less than the best in all you do.

# About the Author

$\mathbf{A}$dam Contos is well suited to guide others on this journey to understand what it takes to start with a win. A master at winning, he's CEO of RE/MAX Holdings Inc., one of the most recognizable real estate brands in the world, which includes RE/MAX, Motto Mortgage/ Motto Franchising Inc., and booj, a real estate technology company.

He's an entrepreneur, as well as a prior Marine, deputy sheriff, and SWAT team leader, who used to kick in doors, blow up things, and save people. He honed his sales skills as an undercover narcotics cop. Now he's traded his badge for the boardroom and works to break down barriers to consensus and leadership, overcome conventional and archaic thinking, and help as many people as possible achieve personal success.

Says Adam: "I choose to start every day with a win—to create habits and build momentum while working toward better opportunities for those I serve. Leadership is about mindset, knowing when to break the rules, why it's important to challenge the status quo, and how to inspire others to achieve their own greatness."

A believer in the notion that people mirror the behavior of their leaders, Adam doesn't just talk the talk—he leads by example. He's a former college dropout who went on to earn an MBA. He's an in-demand speaker, podcaster, and maverick business executive who shares his insights regularly with his *Start With a Win* podcast (www.StartWithAWin.com). He's also a leader who actually does what he encourages others to do, whether it's leading with com-passion, consistency, authenticity, and kindness; showing up at the gym at 5 a.m.; using video and social media to build community; or dropping everything to brighten the day of someone who needs it.

Now, in these pages, he and his knowledge are here for you so that you, too, can start every day with your own wins.

# Index